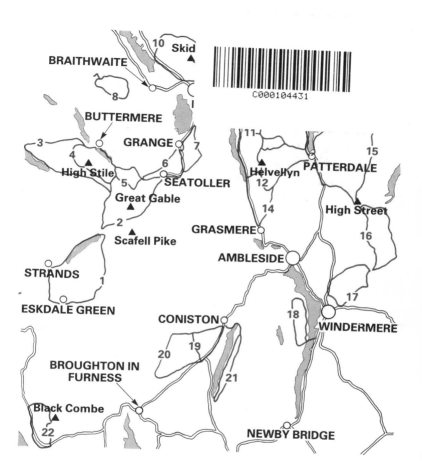

BRAITHWAITE

Skid ▲

10

8

BUTTERMERE

GRANGE

3

4

High Stile ▲

5

7

6

SEATOLLER

Great Gable ▲

2

Scafell Pike ▲

STRANDS

1

ESKDALE GREEN

11

Helvellyn ▲

PATTERDALE

12

14

High Street ▲

GRASMERE

AMBLESIDE

15

16

17

18

WINDERMERE

CONISTON

19

20

21

BROUGHTON IN FURNESS

Black Combe ▲

22

NEWBY BRIDGE

C000104431

MOUNTAIN BIKE GUIDE
The Lake District
The Howgills &
The Yorkshire Dales

by
JEREMY ASHCROFT

ERNEST

Rounding High Pike with Dentdale in the distance

Published by The Ernest Press 1989
©Copyright Jeremy Ashcroft

Reprinted 1990

Ashcroft, Jeremy, <u>1959-</u>
    Mountain bike guide to the Lake District,
    the Howgills & the Yorkshire Dales
    1. Northern England. Mountains. Visitors'
    guides
    914.27'04858

    ISBN 0–948153–10–5

Photograph processing GMT Colour Lab, Lancaster
Typeset by Bureau-Graphics
Printed by Martins of Berwick
Bound by Hunter & Foulis

Contents

ROUTES

Contents(cont)

Acknowledgements

The preparation of this guide book would have been impossible
without the unstinting assistance of many people - I am grateful to
them all. Loraine Iddon for checking the MS and accompanying me
on routes; Chris Betts, for checking the MS, accompanying me on
routes, and for his photographs; Kathryn Eccles, Al Gibson, Phil
Girvin, Alex Gold, Roy Jackson, Harry Webb, Phil Worthington, for
accompanying me on routes; Peter Rodgers of the Lake District National Park and Ray Lonsdale of the Yorkshire Dales National Park
for advice and guidance. I would also like to thank Jim Iddon for the
loan of his computer and Phil McIver of Grange Cycles for technical
assistance.
Jeremy Ashcroft Mewith, January 1989

INTRODUCTION

Within the boundaries of the Lake District National Park and the Yorkshire Dales National Park, there is, without doubt, the greatest potential for mountain biking in this country. There are literally hundreds of miles of 'Rights of Way' open to cyclists across summits, passes, moorland and along valleys. The range of challenges is tremendous. There are easy routes that offer peace and tranquility amongst fine scenery with few technical or navigational problems, then there are the full-blown 'Mountain' bike rides which will test even the most experienced and accomplished riders.

The aim of this guide book is to select and detail the best routes available from the two national parks. Each route meets simple basic criteria, it should be a circular tour and at least 2/3 of the total distance should be rideable; it should also be possible to complete the route within a day. In addition each route is described in the direction which gives the shortest ascent and the longest down hill run. To fully enjoy mountain biking amongst 'real' mountains it is important that you accept a certain amount of pushing or carrying. If you limit yourself solely to routes that can be ridden throughout their entirety then you will close the door on most of the routes in this book and a lot of wonderful experiences.

Like any other activity in the mountains, mountain biking is potentially dangerous. On undertaking any excursion into the mountains you should consider, as far as possible, the level of risk you are prepared to expose yourself to, and if anything went wrong what the consequences would be to yourself and to other people. The sudden changes in weather, precipitous terrain and remoteness from help are all key elements which must be taken seriously. Only attempt routes that you know are within your personal limits - there is nothing more rewarding than returning from a hard day in the hills and knowing at the back of your mind that you still had plenty in reserve.

ENVIRONMENT

Both the Lake District and Yorkshire Dales National Parks are highly sensitive mountain areas that must be treated with the greatest respect if they are to remain unspoilt. Over the last few decades there has been a tremendous increase in the number of people using the areas for recreational purposes, which in some parts of the parks could be seen to have reached saturation point. Apart from the effect which tourism has made upon the area, agriculture and industry have to a similar extent affected the environment. Any new activity like mountain biking which could be perceived to have a detrimental effect will be rightly viewed with suspicion by authorities and other groups with a vested interest.

It is our love for mountains, moors and hills that draws us, as mountain bikers, back time and time again; we seek to enjoy them not destroy them - we know this but others do not. Each individual mountain biker should regard themself as an ambassador of the sport. Your behaviour to the environment and to others in the environment should be impeccable. You should do all in your power to avoid damage by yourself and others. Simple actions can make all the difference

Never ride across ground that can be permanently eroded (ie. bogs, scree etc.) get off and walk or better still find a way round.

Never skid and avoid locking your wheels when breaking.

Set your bike up so that it is equipped sympathetically (e.g. wide tyres for greater surface contact area, resin pedals that deform rather than scratch rocks etc.)

Do not travel in large groups, 5 - 6 should be regarded as the maximum.

Two codes have been estabished which are particularly relevant to mountain biking.

The Off-Road Code
Issued by the Mountain Bike Club

Only ride where you know you have a legal right.
Always yield to horses and pedestrians.
Avoid animals and crops. In some circumstances this may not be possible, at which times contact should be kept to a minimum.

Take all litter with you.
Leave all gates as found.
Keep the noise down.
Don't get annoyed with anyone, it never solves any problems.
Always try to be self-sufficient, for you and your bike.
Never create a fire hazard.

The Country Code
Issued by the Countryside Commission

Enjoy the countryside and respect its life and work.
Guard against all risk of fire.
Fasten all gates.
Keep your dogs under close control.
Keep to public paths across farmland.
Use gates and stiles to cross fences, hedges and walls.
Leave livestock, crops and machinery alone.
Take your litter home.
Help keep all water clean.
Protect wildlife, plants and trees.
Take special care on country roads.
Make no unnecessary noise.

RIGHTS OF WAY

Off-road cyclists have right of way on virtually all public bridleways
and other tracks of higher status (e.g. BOAT - by-way open to all
traffic and RUPP - road used as a public path). On bridleways cyclists
must give way to walkers and horse riders and on all rights of way
it is an offence to cycle recklessly, carelessly and under the influence
of drink! There is no right of way for cyclists on public foot paths.
   Although every care has been taken in the production and
checking of this guide book there will inevitably be misinterpreta-
tions and information relating to the status of rights of way will
change with passage of time. Therefore the representation in this
guide book of any route is no evidence of the existence of right of
way. If you are in any doubt you can check the Definitive Maps
which are held by the appropriate County Council or National Park
Authority

If you are asked by a landowner or occupier to leave the land or route you are on because you are thought to be trespassing, do so by the shortest practicable route, as quickly as you can. Do not seek confrontation, it will achieve nothing; if you believe you have right of way check with the local authorities and get them to pursue the matter - if you cause undue friction mountain biking will suffer.

Further information can be found in *Cycling Off-Road and the Law* issued by the Cyclist's Touring Club.

MAPS

This guide book is specifically designed to be used with a map and not by itself. Although there are numerous proprietary maps avaliable the Ordnance Survey maps are the only real alternative. They provide precise cartographic information and are constantly being updated.

At the beginning of each route the relevant Ordnance Survey 1:25 000 or 1:50 000 scale maps are listed. The Lake District is also covered by 1:63 360 (1 inch to 1 mile) scale map which because of its limited detail cannot be recommended for anything other than route planning. It is always a good idea to have the map folded to the right area in a map case or a clear plastic bag. Even in the best conditions there is always a breeze that will make reading the map and refolding it difficult.

EQUIPMENT

The Bike

The type of mountain bike you use is of course a highly personal thing but if you are going to take it into "real" mountain bike country it should be as light as possible, mechanically sound with effective brakes and unclutterd. Mud guards, racks and bottle cages are OK on the road but are a waste of time in the hills - adding to weight and susceptible to damage, they cause no end of problems. Tyres with at least a 2 ins. section should be fitted as they have a large contact surface area, minimising any damage to soft ground. At some point on all the routes you are likely to have to carry your bike so it is essential that you pad the frame accordingly. Closed-cell foam is about the best, it is waterproof, cheap, comfortable and keeps its shape well - you cannot really overdo the padding particularly if you are attempting a route that involves sustained carrying.

Carry a basic tool kit and spares so that you can·make adjustments and repairs but don't go over the top - remember you have to carry all your equipment.

The Biker

Navigation and Survival; regardless of whatever else you take with you, the following items should be regarded as essential and you should be fully familiar with their use:

Map - relevant to the area! **Compass**.

Survival Bag (8ft x 4ft 500 gauge polythene bag).

Whistle - International Alpine Distress Signal - six blasts followed by a pause of a minute then a repetition.

Torch - International Alpine Distress Signal - six flashes followed by a pause of a minute then a repetition of the six flashes.

Emergency rations.

Clothing

Normal cycling clothing is worse than useless for the range of conditions that you will encounter amongst this country's hills and mountains. Skin tops and shorts simply do not offer the level of protection to keep you warm and dry, and touring shoes do not give enough grip or support. In selecting clothing it is better to choose from the large range designed for climbers and walkers. A layer system is the best approach as this will allow you to strip or dress according to the conditions or whether you are moving or at rest. Essentially the combination of clothes you choose should be windproof, waterproof and insulate even when wet. Use a rucksack or bum bag to carry clothes and equipment so that if you become separated from your bike your hands are free from carrying panniers, saddle bags etc.

Conditions will also dictate footwear but generally it should have good grip (Vibram or Skywalker type soles are about the best) and should support both the foot and the ankle. If you decide to wear training shoes (not recommended particularly for beginners) you should use the type designed for fell runners - some compounds used in the soles of training shoes are lethal on wet grass and rock. Whether you wear a helmet or not is a serious decision that can only be made by you. If you do decide to wear one, the lightweight type used by climbers offer the best protection in the tumbling falls likely to be encountered in the hills. In this situation soft lightweight cycling helmets are likely to break-up and give only limited protection.

ACCIDENT PROCEDURE

Do any immediate First Aid that is necessary. Stop any bleeding by applying clean dressings and bandaging firmly. If the patient is unconscious, make sure that he is not choking with his tongue blocking the back of his throat.

Make the patient as comfortable as possible and treat for shock. Keep him warm, putting spare clothing etc. as insulation underneath him. Warm sweet drinks should be given to those who are conscious and suffering from exhaustion or exposure. Never give drinks to anyone with chest, abdominal or head injuries, or any injured patient who may be transported to hospital quickly and put under an anaesthetic. If a long carry of many hours is expected, then warm sugary drinks may be a life saver in case of shock and when no morphia is avaliable. (For further advice see the section on First Aid.)

Give the international Alpine Distress Signal - six blasts on a whistle (or six shouts or flashes of a torch) followed by a pause of a minute then a repetition of the six blasts, shouts or whistles. Keep giving this signal system. If your signals are eventually heard you should hear an answering whistle - three blasts followed by a pause of a minute, repeated several times. If by chance your whistle or torch is missing and your voice doesn't carry because of the wind, you can wave a white or coloured cloth.

If your signal does not produce assistance, one or two (if possible) of the party must go down and contact the Police or the nearest Mountain Rescue Post. You should already be familiar with these; they may be marked on maps, though locations sometimes change and should be checked. The messenger must carry and give the following information concerning the accident.

Exact position, giving six-figure grid reference or, if this is not feasible, as much information as possible to enable a rescue party to go straight to the injured person.

Time of the accident.
How many people are injured.
Nature of the injuries.

If the injured person has to be left alone whilst you fetch help, first give him all your spare clothing to keep him warm. If his injuries permit, move him to a good sheltered position, otherwise erect a windbreak around him. It may be many hours before a rescue party reaches him, the weather may worsen and he may easily die of shock and exposure in the meantime unless you take very careful precautions.

If he is conscious, reassure him, leave him a torch and whistle to guide the rescue party to his aid. If unconscious, belay him to a rock if possible to prevent from falling further or from wandering off in a dazed condition if he gains consciousness. It is wise to leave a cheering message before you leave him in case he should regain consciousness. If possible mark the position of the patient with a bright piece of clothing or equipment. A cairn of stones will be better than no position mark at all.

When you have done everything possible for the patient go and fetch help, descending quickly but carefully.

First Aid
Every party on the hills should carry a first aid pack. This should contain as a minimum:
Plasters (for blisters and cuts); lint or gauze (for dressings, etc);
Acriflavine cream (antiseptic and soothing cream useful for burns, cuts, etc); and a selection of bandages.
Salt is a very useful commodity in mountains and may sometimes relieve cramp. A solution of salt makes a good dressing for cuts, burns and sprains.

Treatment

Medical treatment is obviously best left in the hands of a doctor or someone highly skilled in first aid but, if an accident does occur, it may be necessary for an unskilled person to give immediate first aid before a rescue party can be summoned. Every mountain biker should therefore learn at least the rudiments of First Aid, and this can be done through the St. John Ambulance Association, the British Red Cross Society or, in Scotland, the St. Andrew's Ambulance Association.

The notes below are intended purely as a simple guide for laymen faced with a mountain accident.

General Principles

Check the airway. Check it frequently and keep it clear...Stop any bleeding and apply dressing to open wounds...Do not move the patient unless you are quite sure that there is no injury to the spine...Treat for shock. Keep warm and relieve pain...Immobilize broken limbs to relieve pain and prevent any further damage...Do not experiment. When in doubt, do as little First Aid as possible since an unskilled person can do considerable damage by applying the wrong treatment.

Shock

Shock is present in almost all cases of accident. The symptoms are pallor, weak and rapid pulse, cold, clammy skin, and hunger for air. Make the patient comfortable and insulate him from the cold ground. Reassure him, allay anxiety and relieve pain. Never overheat a shocked patient.

Burns and Scalds

Use a dry sterile dressing on a wound and treat the patient for pain and shock. Leave any adhering clothing on a burn. Remove hot wet clothing from a scald.

Cuts and Wounds

Cut away clothing to make sure there is no dangerous bleeding if it is suspected. Stop any bleeding by applying direct pressure on the wound with a clean dressing or pad and then a bandage.

Sprained, Twisted and Dislocated Ankles

In general, do not remove boot - it forms an excellent splint and sufficient relief from swelling can usually be obtained by loosening the laces. If boot is removed apply cold compress and bandage firmly to limit swelling.

Cramp

Massage the affected part and apply warmth. It may sometimes be relieved by drinking a salt solution or eating a few grains.

Frostbite

Early or superficial frostbite is best treated by applying body warmth or breathing on the cold parts until sensation returns. The warm skin of the crutch or the armpit is good or if possible immersing the part in warm water. Once a frostbitten part has been rewarmed, keep it warm. Do not rub. Treatment of deep or established frostbite should be delayed until hospital treatment can be given. Protect the parts from rubbing or banging for the tissue is devitalised and will readily tear.

Snakebite

The only poisonous snake in Britain is the adder, but it is a frequenter of hill districts. The commonest symptoms are fright and fear of death. Reassurance is vital. Death from snake bite is extremely rare. Keep the patient at rest. Immobilize the bitten part as for a fracture and apply a firm bandage on the heart side of the bite. Administer analgesia (eg. asprin) but no morphia.

Fractures

Fractures must be immobilized before the patient is carried down on stretcher, but if you have no experience or training in First Aid, it is probably better not to try to immobilize a fracture before the Rescue Party arrives, unless it is causing the patient extreme pain. Do not try to straighten a broken limb.

Arm. Bandage the upper arm to the chest (if splints are avaliable, first bandage these to the arm), and either put the forearm in a sling or bandage it also to the chest, whichever is more comfortable for the patient.

Leg. Bandage the injured leg to the sound one at the ankles, knees and hips, padding well between the knees, or bandage the leg to a splint if available. Avoid moving the injured leg and do not try to straighten.

Collar Bone. Place the hand near the other collar bone and bandage the whole shoulder and arm to the chest.

Spine. On no account move the patient. A spinal injury is often difficult to diagnose, but signs are pain in the back or numbness in the legs. If in the slightest doubt, treat as a spinal injury, and do not move until you have plenty of helpers and a proper stretcher.

Neck. Carefully lay the patient flat on his back. Place a pair of boots, one on each side of the head, with the soles facing outwards and the uppers crossing under the nape of the neck. Narrow triangular bandages can then be tied firmly round the boots and head across the forehead and chin.

Jaw. Support the jaw with the hand, then bandage. Don't allow the patient to lie back or he will choke as he cannot swallow.

Head Injuries

Check the airway frequently and keep it clear. Stop any bleeding by applying a sterile pad and bandage firmly, then place the patient in the recovery position.

Unconscious Patient

Do not administer drinks or morphia. Make sure breathing is unobstructed and remove any dentures. Turn the patient on his side in the coma position to prevent the tongue falling back and obstructing the airway and to help the drainage of secretions.

Heat Exhaustion

Reduce temperature by moving into cool shade, using cold water and/or helping respiration by increasing air movement - fanning. Apply preventive action - i.e. the giving of salt in solution.

Exposure

Exposure is caused by exhaustion and severe chilling of the body surface, usually in windy and wet conditions. This is one of the most common reasons for rescue calls in mountains and must be guarded

against continually. Additional information can be found in Mountain Hypothermia, issued by the British Mountaineering Council.

Signs and Symptoms:
Complaints of cold, tiredness, cramp.
Mental and physical lethargy.
Lack of understanding of simple questions and directions.
Slurring speech.
Irrational or violent behaviour.
Abnormality of vision.
Collapse and coma.
These may not all be present nor in the order given.
　All cases should be treated immediately, for mild cases can rapidly become very serious. Suspect others, and yourself, of being mild cases and protect the party from being reduced to the same condition.

Prevention:
Wear good clothing including windproof and waterproof garments. Avoid getting overtired. Do not go too long without energy-giving foods.If any member of a party is becoming tired, cold and wet, the group should go down into a more sheltered area.

Treatment:
Stop. Provide shelter from the elements causing exposure. Having found a sheltered spot, put up a tent or use the emergency bivouac provided by rucksack and 8ft x 4ft 500 gauge polythene bag. Give the patient prolonged rest. Immediately insulate the patient from further heat loss. Insulation from the cold ground is particularly important. Cover for head, face and neck is a great help. Place the patient in a horizontal position and if possible place a warm companion alongside him. Anxiety and mental stress is often an important contributory factor. Be cheerful and encouraging. If there is no breathing in severe cases, mouth to mouth resuscitation should be given until normal breathing is obtained. Do not rub the patient to restore circulation. Do not allow further exertion and thereby use up essential energy. Do not give alcohol.
If in doubt send for help but prompt action, good equipment and

good leadership will provide the important safeguards against exposure.

The sections on Accident Procedure and First Aid were reproduced with the kind permisson of the Britsh Mountaineering Council from their excellent booklet Safety on Mountains.

THE ROUTES

Generally the routes fit into three main categories - valley routes, those that cross passes, and those that visit summits. When selecting a route you should carefully balance your experience and fitness against its grade, distance and height gain. Only attempt routes that are within your personal limits. Rapid weather changes, navigational errors, accidents and mechanical problems are all the more difficult to deal with if you have pushed yourself too much and attempted a route beyond your capability.

Times

The times given for each route are generally fast and are based on a fit competent party with the benefit of good conditions. Lack of experience and poor conditions can greatly extend the time needed to complete a route; this should be taken into account before commencing - particularly in winter when the daylight hours are short.

Grades

Each route has been graded according to its technical difficulty. Adjectives have been used to describe how an experienced mountain biker new to the district would assess the levels of difficulty encountered.

Easy - no significant difficulties
Moderate - mostly good going but with some difficulties
Difficult - more sustained difficulties
Very Difficult - routes across the harder passes and that reach easier summits
Severe - routes that reach summits and cross very dangerous terrain
Very Severe - the limit of feasible mountain biking at this time!
The grades selected for each route have been agreed only by the

limited number of people involved in the production of this guide book. Until a grading system has been firmly established and recognized by a broad spectrum of mountain bikers the grades listed can be nothing more than subjective.

Abbreviations

E	East
ft	Feet
L	Left (used in relation to the direction of travel)
m	Miles
N	North
NE	North East
NW	North West
O.S.	Ordnance Survey
R	Right (used in relation to the direction of travel)
S	South
SE	South East
SW	South West
W	West
yds	Yards
°	Degrees from north

ILLUSTRATIONS

Each route is illustrated by either a map or a relief map, a photograph and in some cases a line illustration. Generally a straightforward map is used to show the course of a route, but where steep complicated terrain dictates, a relief map has been used instead. There is no consistency in scale as it was considered more important to show the whole route on either a single page or a two page spread - eliminating the need to turn pages to see the whole route. The photographs and line illustrations are to highlight interesting features and to give an idea of the character of particular routes.

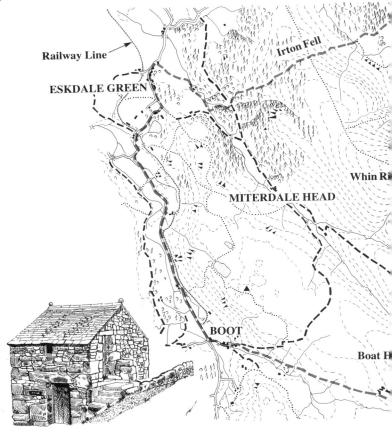

Railway Line

ESKDALE GREEN

Irton Fell

Whin Ri

MITERDALE HEAD

BOOT

Boat H

Eskdale and Wasdale

Grade: Difficult - Time: 4½ Hours - Height Gain: 1590ft
Distance: 14 Miles - 6 off road, 8 on road
Terrain: Valleys and mountain passes
Surface: Generally well graded tracks with some steep rocky sections
Start Point Grid Reference: 127039, Strands (Nether Wasdale)
Map: O.S The English Lakes 1:25 000 SW sheet

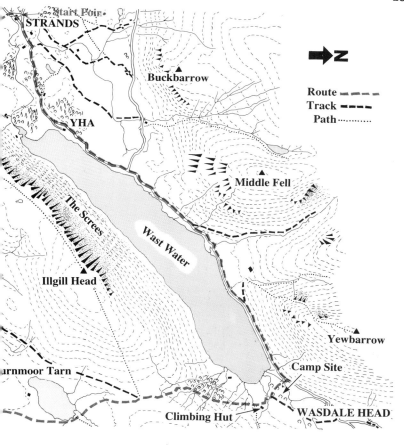

On the western flank of Scafell is a wide depression occupied by Burnmoor Tarn; further west again is Illgill Head and Miterdale - together these features seperate Wasdale from Eskdale. A circular tour can be completed by taking the well trodden bridleway from Wasdale Head to Boot via Burnmoor Tarn; then down Eskdale to Eskdale Green where the Miterdale road joins a bridleway over Irton Fell and leads back to Wasdale. The route does involve a fair amount of road work; but what road work there is, is more than made up for by the diverse scenery and the excellent off-road sections, particularly the descent from Burnmoor Tarn.

Route Description

From Strands (Nether Wasdale) take the road to Wasdale Head and follow it for 3m until just past the head of Wastwater a R turn can be taken for the camp site (National Trust). Follow the track past the camp site and continue along it as it turns R near the climbing hut at Brackenclose and crosses a bridge. The track crosses another beck and climbs the fell side S above Fence Wood. Continue along it to the col above Burnmoor Tarn ignoring the paths that break off R to Illgill Head and Miterdale. A short descent leads to Burnmoor Tarn. Cross the bridge at the outlet beck and follow the track as it gradually climbs for ½m S. Stay quite high above Whillan Beck and don't be tempted to take the path down to it. The gradient soon eases and the track becomes more obvious on the ground. Continue S and make the fast descent down to Boot. The track ends at a bridge by an old mill; cross it and join the road through the hamlet to a junction with the main valley road.

From the T junction at Boot turn R and head down Eskdale to another junction opposite the King George IV Hotel.(Following by the side of the road down Eskdale is a narrow gauge railway that runs a regular service in summer - with both steam and diesel trains.) Turn R at the junction and follow the road to Eskdale Green. Pass through the hamlet and take the first road on the R; follow it for ½m up Miterdale and take the bridleway for Irton Pike on the L at a bridge over the River Mite. The bridleway winds its way up through the woods of Irton Fell to emerge on an open ridge after 700ft of ascent. All that remains now is to ride straight (NW) over the crest and make the very steep descent back down to Strands - worth testing your brakes before you start this one!

The Screes, Wasdale

TOUR OF GREAT GABLE

N

Route — — — —
Track - - - -
Path ....

Car Park
GATESGARTH
Fleetwith Pike
Scarth Gap Pass
▲ Hay Stacks
YHA
Pillar ▲
Brandre
Black Sail Pass
Kirk Fell
Great Gable
WASDALE HEAD

Napes Needle

Tour of Great Gable

Grade: Severe - Time: 6 Hours - Height Gain: 4000ft
Distance: 14 Miles - 9 off road, 5 on road
Terrain: High mountain passes
Surface: Steep roads and steep but generally well graded mountain tracks
with some rock steps
Start Point Grid Reference: 244138, Seatoller
Maps: O.S. The English Lakes 1:25 000 NW and SW sheets

ROSTHWAITE

YHA

Car Park

YHA

Start Point

nister Pass

SEATOLLER

SEATHWAITE

e Brown

Glaramara

Styhead Tarn

Sprinkling Tarn

Stockley Bridge

Great Gable, not the highest peak in Lakeland, but undoubtedly the best known and best loved. Its summit is reached by thousands of walkers every year, its popular crags were the birthplace of British rock climbing and its form is used in the badge of the Lake District National Park. Fortunately although there is no right of way to its summit for mountain bikers there is a system of passes that surround it which are crossed by bridleways forming a circular route which takes in all of Great Gable's aspects. The passes in question are Honister to the north east, Scarth Gap and Black Sail to the north west and Styhead to the south east. The crossing of each individually is a worthwhile experience but linked together they constitute a classic tour around the heart of Lakeland. Completion of this tour is not an easy undertaking for although navigation is not a problem, considerable height gain, overall distance and some difficult terrain make it quite a testing ride.

The tour can be started from either Borrowdale, Buttermere, Ennerdale or Wasdale and in either direction; but the best bet is to start from Borrowdale. This has two advantages; firstly the road section over Honister Pass can quickly be dispensed with and secondly the short steep section over Black Sail Pass can be attacked in ascent where you would have to carry anyway - thus leaving all the rideable section for descent.

Route Description

From the car park at Seatoller, Borrowdale take the road over Honister Pass for just under 4m to Gatesgarth; turn L after the farm and follow the bridleway across the valley at the head of Buttermere. Cross the bridge and follow the track through a zig-zag and then S as it gradually climbs the fells of Warnscale to Scarth Gap - the track is steep in parts but generally not difficult. Near the top of the pass the gradient starts to ease and it is possible to ride over the crest. Continue S over Scarth Gap and descend into Ennerdale; the track gradually steepens until just above the forest edge some earth and boulder steps are encountered; negotiate the steps and follow the edge of the forest avoiding the low overhanging branches - not easy! The track then joins the forest road; take it as it leads slightly up hill to the YHA's Black Sail Hut. The N face of Great Gable can clearly be seen from the hut with its dark crags dominating the head of Ennerdale.

To reach Black Sail Pass continue along the track past the hut SE to a ford and bridge and then S as it skirts the forest edge (tree felling was going on when this route was checked). Follow the track as it climbs the steep fell side by Sail Beck and over an awkward rock step at which point it leaves the beck and zig-zags to the top of the pass. Again as you near the top of the pass the gradient eases and it is possible to ride. From Black Sail Pass there are spectacular views across Mosedale to Red Pike and Yewbarrow. You are now at the halfway point and the start of the best down hill run of the route (change from the The English Lakes NW to The English Lakes SW O.S. map). The track drops SW then S into Mosedale over ideal mountain bike terrain and leads after 2m to Wasdale Head. Follow it easily at first from the pass over a short series of rock steps then down a fast stony section. The track then zig-zags steeply down to a ford which crosses Gatherstone Beck, traverses the rough lower slopes of Kirk Fell and then opens out onto the valley floor. Keep an eye out to the SE for Scafell; it starts to come into view at this point. Continue easily down Mosedale crossing a few entertaining fords to a junction with the track from Burnthwaite. The next section up to Sty Head starts here but it is worth continuing S a short way and making a slight detour to Wasdale Head and the Hotel.

At all times whilst crossing Black Sail Pass, Great Gable has remained hidden by Kirk Fell but once Wasdale Head is reached its S face can be seen in total. Running across the steep screes of the S face is an unlikely looking track which makes a rising traverse to Sty Head - a col set between Great Gable and Great End. This track is gained by backtracking to the junction turning R and heading E past the farm at Burnthwaite until after 1m a bridge is crossed. Continue along the side of Lingmell Beck until the track splits. Take the L branch which steadily traverses the screes and climbs some awkward outcrops before levelling then descending slightly to Sty Head (Mountain Rescue Box). High above this track are the Napes Crags and Napes Needle which were first climbed by W.P. Haskett-Smith in 1886. It is possible to take the R branch to Sty Head but it is not as inspiring and has a very steep last section.

Sty Head is an important access point to the surrounding peaks with numerous paths and tracks heading off in all directions. Head NE over some boggy ground until you pick up a stony track past Styhead Tarn. Continue NE and follow the course of Styhead Gill first on the L bank and then, after the bridge, on the R bank with rough going through boulders to a small wood perched above Taylorgill Force. The track now leaves the Gill and heads E steeply down the fell side to Stockley Bridge. From Stockley Bridge take the good track N to Seathwaite and then the road for 1½m back to Seatoller.

Overleaf right: Descending into Mosedale (Wasdale) – Scafell in the distance.

Overleaf left: The N. face of Great Gable from the head of Ennerdale.

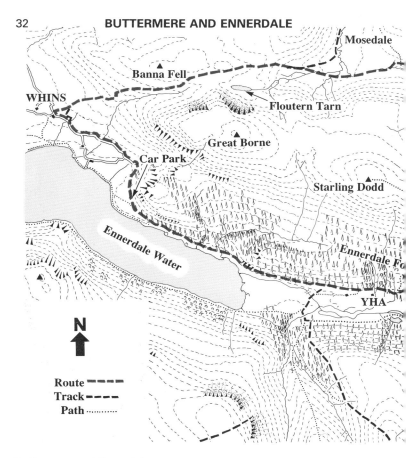

WHINS

Mosedale

Banna Fell

Floutern Tarn

Great Borne

Car Park

Starling Dodd

Ennerdale Water

Ennerdale Fo

YHA

N

Route — — —
Track - - - -
Path ....

Buttermere and Ennerdale

Grade: Difficult - Time: 5-5½ Hours - Height Gain: 2000ft
Distance: 16 Miles - 15 off road, 1 on road
Terrain: High mountain passes
Surface: Steep rocky mountain tracks, good forest tracks and boggy moorland
Start Point Grid Reference: 196150, Gatesgarth
Map: O.S. The English Lakes 1:25 000 NW sheet

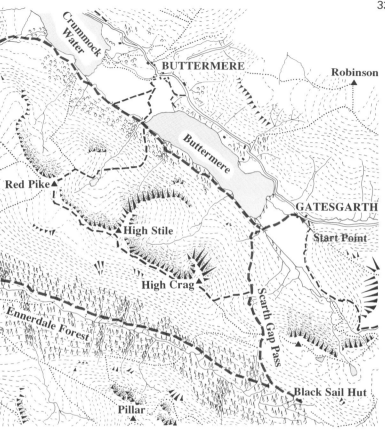

Access to most Lakeland valleys can be gained by car or coach, which, particularly in the summer months, bring throngs of trippers getting little further than the prepared picnic sites and car parks. If you feel like cycling the length of a valley, without the presence of noise and fumes, then Ennerdale is the place to go; motor vehicles apart from those on business are restricted. Admittedly the character of Ennerdale has been changed by the Forestry Commision's plantations but this apart the surrounding mountains make a spectacular scene. To the south Pillar, Kirk Fell and Great Gable form a long wall of high crags which only relent in height at cols on either side of Kirk Fell. To the north the fells of Great Borne, Starling Dodd and the High Stile range lack the wild craggy aspect but are similar in height. Access to the long run down Ennerdale can be gained by crossing Scarth Gap from Buttermere with a return leg made via the lonely Floutern Tarn.

Route Description

From the side of the farm at Gatesgarth follow the bridleway across the valley floor at the head of Buttermere. Cross the bridge and follow the track through a zig-zag and then S as it gradually climbs the fells of Warnscale to Scarth Gap - the track is steep in parts but generally not difficult. Near the top of the pass the gradient starts to ease and it is possible to ride over the crest. Continue S over Scarth Gap and descend into Ennerdale; the track gradually steepens until just above the forest edge some earth and boulder steps are encountered; negotiate the steps and follow the edge of the forest avoiding the low overhanging branches - not easy! The track then joins the forest road which is worth following SE a short distance to Black Sail Hut - one of the best placed youth hostels in the area. The N face of Great Gable can clearly be seen from the hut with its dark crags dominating the head of Ennerdale.

From Black Sail Hut backtrack and follow the forest road NW down Ennerdale; the riding is easy being mostly downhill - it is worth making frequent stops as there are clearings with good views of Pillar Rock. After 6m the road and car park are reached at Bowness on the edge of Ennerdale Water. Follow the road for 1¼m to a junction at Whins where a R turn can be made and the bridleway to Floutern Pass joined. Continue E up the lane as the track climbs steadily across Banna Fell above Gill Beck (numerous signs indicate past access disputes; so make sure you stay on the bridleway). The surrounding fells are grassy and quite open, gradually easing in gradient as the top of the pass is reached, allowing pleasant riding above Floutern Tarn. From the tarn continue E and cross the flat boggy moorland at the head of Mosedale and descend towards Crummock Water. Once you reach Black Beck stay on the L side until the gradient eases and you can ford it just below a sheepfold (the track is very boggy and vague on the ground). Continue along the track towards Crummock and follow it as it skirts the shore and heads SE along Buttermere Dubs (river between the two lakes) to Buttermere. Once Buttermere is reached the track climbs slightly into Burtness Wood but soon descends again and is followed easily back to the bridge crossed at the start of the tour. From the bridge take the track back across the valley to Gatesgarth.

Buttermere from Scarth Gap track

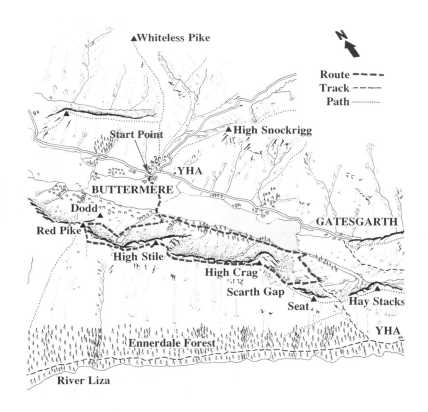

The High Stile Range

Grade: Very Severe - **Time:** 4-4½ Hours - **Height Gain:** 2673ft
Distance: 6½ Miles all off road
Terrain: High craggy mountains
Surface: Very difficult going with scree, boulders, exposed crags and steep ascents and descents
Start Point Grid Reference: 174170, Buttermere
Map: O.S. The English Lakes 1:25 000 NW sheet

For mountain bikers a traverse of the High Stile Range is probably the hardest legal undertaking Lakeland has to offer; and is very near the limit of what is feasible on a bike. This high craggy ridge of mountains forms a formidable barrier to the south west of Buttermere; with approaches at each end that are both steep and loose, making ascent and descent with a bike very difficult. The ridge consists of three main summits; High Stile the highest in the centre at 2644ft, Red Pike to the north west and High Crag to the south east, both respectivly a little lower. Strewn with boulders and craggy outcrops the ridge maintains a consistent height providing interesting riding in a magnificent setting above the surrounding valleys of Buttermere and Ennerdale.

Route Description

From Buttermere village follow the bridleway past the Bridge Hotel and the Fish Hotel easily round a farm lane to a bridge at the outlet of Buttermere. At this point there is some confusion as several tracks and paths meet; you should follow around the corner of the lake and pick up the bridleway that climbs steeply up through the woods onto the open fell side of Old Burtness. Impressively constructed the track zig-zags up the hill side. Follow it as it contours W and meets Sour Milk Gill; from here it takes the course of the gill. Continue along it as it first follows above the Gill on the L bank, crosses it then follows above the gill on the R bank until it emerges from Bleaberry Tarn (crossing the gill is easy as the gill runs beneath boulders and scree in its upper reaches). At Bleaberry Tarn the track can clearly be seen (red scree) as it climbs steeply up the R side of the corrie wall to The Saddle and then through some crags to the summit of Red Pike. Follow it but take care amongst the crags as there are numerous routes some of which climb through tight chimneys and exposed steps.

The ridge extends SE for 2½m over High Stile to High Crag and is easy to follow requiring only a few detours around crags and gully heads. In bad weather navigation can be a problem as various paths lead out onto subsiduary ridges and ultimately over big crags. The simplest approach is to head SW (always taking the right fork) and avoid paths heading NE - easier said than done!

The descent SE down Gamlin End is very steep and loose and takes someone with a long neck and small brain to complete without dismounting! Things do ease a bit as a col is reached; at which point the route turns left and descends steeply over grass and boulders (very indistinct) to meet the track descending from Scarth Gap. Take this track as it descends N to a junction of bridleways and the valley floor. Turn L and take the higher of two tracks above the lake shore through the woods. This leads easily back to the bridge crossed at the start of the route, and then on into Buttermere village.

Overleaf left: Descent from Scarth Gap; the easiest part of the High Stile route.

Warnscale Bottom

Grade: Very Difficult - Time: 2-2½ Hours - Height Gain: 1425ft
Distance: 5 Miles - 3 off road, 2 on road
Terrain: High craggy fells
Surface: Steep quarry road or erosion protected path, open fells, steep
loose and terraced track, steep metalled road
Start point grid reference: 225136, Honister Pass
Map: O.S. The English Lakes 1:25 000 NW sheet

Overleaf right: Descending into Warnscale Bottom.

Tucked away behind Gatesgarth in Buttermere is the impressively propor-
tioned corrie of Warnscale Bottom. From its head at a col between Fleetwith
Pike and Hay Stacks descends an old quarry track that winds its way to the
corrie floor, first following above the course of Warnscale Beck waterfalls;
then crossing the steep precipitous slopes of Fleetwith Pike on a cleverly
constructed terrace. The passage of time has taken toll on this old quarrying
track; streams have washed parts away and rocks have tumbled into it,
leaving a veritable mine-field of obstacles; combine these with the track's
steepness and you have an excellent mountain bike test-piece - very
technical and not without danger! Although relatively short this route has
a special appeal.

Route Description

By starting at the top of Honister Pass you will be able to get to grips with
the off-road work straight away - work being the operative word, because
to gain the col below Fleetwith Pike you will make a 600ft ascent. There are
two options both of which start behind the quarry buildings at the top of the
pass. Either follow the quarry road which traverses NW towards Honister
Crags and then zig-zags back towards the W; this track is rideable but will
require considerable tenacity as the hairpin bends are steep - you also run
the risk of meeting quarry lorries head on! Alternatively you can follow a
recently diverted track which steeply zig-zags up the hillside forcing a
carry; then follows the course of an old tramway W. Both routes meet at
Dubs quarry near a climbing hut, which is a ½m W of the col and not to be
confused with the old quarrying hut near the col.

From the side of the climbing hut the route can clearly be seen
descending into Warnscale Bottom on the right hand side of Warnscale
Beck. Follow this, easily at first over a few rock steps. The route then starts
to get very technical, steep rock steps and loose rocky slopes are encountered at the edge of a gorge and waterfalls - not the place to lock your front
wheel! Things start to ease a little as the track heads away from the beck and
traverses the slopes of Fleetwith Pike in a great descending arc along a
terrace; but don't relax too much as the difficulties are not over, numerous
boulders and washouts force tricky manoeuvres in exposed hazardous po-
sitions. After ½m a zig-zag signals the end of the real difficulties and a fast
easy track is then followed to Gatesgarth. Turn right and follow the road
back up Honister Pass - the challenge of many a road cyclist!

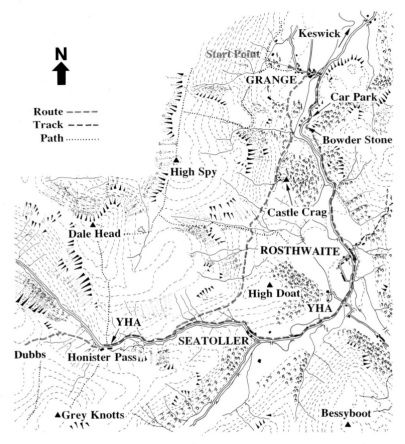

Honister Pass and Castle Crag

Grade: Moderate - Time: 2½ Hours - Height Gain: 900ft
Distance: 8 Miles - 3 off road, 5 on road
Terrain: Craggy wooded valley and a high road pass
Surface: Steep road and stony but well graded track
Start Point Grid Reference: 253175, Grange
Map: O.S. The English Lakes 1:25 000 NW sheet

Castle Crag sits square in the jaws of Borrowdale; viewed from Grange its wooded craggy ramparts seem to block further access up the valley. This of course is a facade and there are two routes that pass its defences. To the east the valley road clings tightly to the course of the River Derwent, breaking out across meadows to Rosthwaite and then makes a steep climb to Honister Pass via Seatoller. To the west a bridleway takes a route through Hollows Farm over the col between Castle Crag and Goat Crag on the slopes of High Spy and then climbs to Honister Pass via another col above High Doat. By making an ascent of Honister Pass on the road then returning to Grange via the bridleway an excellent short tour can be completed - with lots of interesting diversions for exploration and sightseeing. For those wanting to progress from easier routes this tour is a good option.

Route Description

From the junction at Grange take the valley road S into Borrowdale for ½m to a car park and turning on the L; take the track which leads after a short pull to the Bowder Stone - a 2000 ton boulder that probably has its origins amongst the crags above. Continue past the Bowder Stone and descend the rocky track back to the road. Follow the road for 2½m through Rosthwaite to Seatoller and the start of the climb up Honister Pass. The first part of the climb is steep but eases after ¾m allowing a breather before the final short pull to the top of the Pass.

The bridleway back to Grange actually starts ½m back down the road, but if you are feeling energetic a short but steep detour can be made to Dubs Quarry on the col to the W of Honister Pass. Behind the quarry buildings follow the quarry road as it traverses NW towards Honister Crags and then zig-zags back towards the W. The top of the col is a broad expanse which is worth crossing to have a look down into Warnscale Bottom and across to the High Stile Range. Return to the top of the col and take the descent back down the quarry road; fast and very loose - watch out for quarry lorries as it is still in use.

Backtrack ½m down the road towards Seatoller until a L turn can be made onto a bridleway (just before a cattle grid). Follow the track as it contours round the fell to a col between High Doat and Dale Head. From this point make a short climb over the col and ignore the paths that temptingly drop down towards Rosthwaite. Once the col is crossed the track again becomes clear and is followed down for 2m of exciting riding past Castle Crag and through a couple of fords in Dalt Wood to Grange.

Overleaf left: Descent toward Borrowdale from Honister Pass.

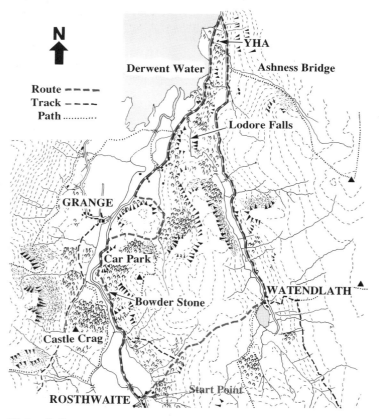

Watendlath

Grade: Easy Time: 2 Hours Height Gain: 1100ft
Distance: 7½ Miles - 2½ off road, 5 on road.
Terrain: Valleys and low fells
Surface: Pleasant valley roads (busy in summer), and erosion protected bridleways.
Start Point Grid Reference: 258149, Rosthwaite
Maps: O.S. The English Lakes 1:25 000 NW sheet

Overleaf right: The track past Castle Crag, Borrowdale.

Borrowdale is a marvellous place to be; its crags, woodland, rivers and lake make for an ideal setting; the epitome of Lakeland. Enjoyed by climbers, walkers and tourists the valleys attractions are renowned - so much so that the picture post cards of Ashness Bridge and the Bowder Stone must be all-time best sellers! This route is unashamedly easy being mostly on tarmac and with few problems encountered on the off-road sections, reserve this ride for a lazy day and be a tourist - take in the sights.

Route Description

Rising to the E of Rosthwaite is a low ridge of fine craggy fells; passing over this ridge is a bridleway that crosses to Watendlath at a low point between Grange Fell and Great Crag. Take the bridleway which crosses Stoneth-waite Beck on the N side of Rosthwaite and follow it as it climbs NE straight up the fell side to the ridge crest. Continue NE over the ridge and drop down to Watendlath via the rocky track past Watendlath Tarn. Follow the road N down the valley for 2½m to a car park and clearing just up from Ashness Bridge. Through the trees at the back of the clearing is a rock promontory which gives a spectacular view over Derwent Water of Skiddaw. Continue down the road over Ashness Bridge and turn sharp L at the junction with the B5289. Head back up Borrowdale for 2m until it is possible to turn L and make a short detour along a bridleway into the small valley of Troutdale. Follow the bridleway as it climbs and skirts around the back of Grange Crags and then drops steeply back to the B5289. Continue along the road for ½m to a car park where another detour can be taken to the Bowder Stone and then back to the road to Rosthwaite.

Overleaf left: Surprise View, Borrowdale.

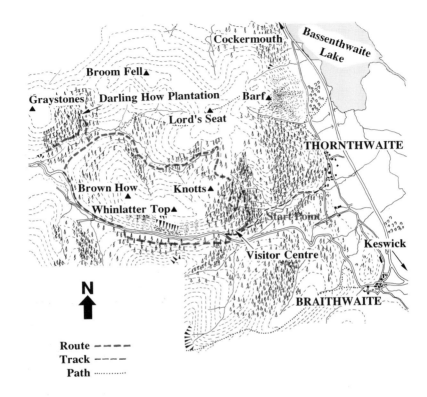

Whinlatter Pass and Thornthwaite Forest

Grade: Easy - Time: 1½ Hours - Height Gain: 1025ft
Distance: 6 Miles - 5 off road, 1 on road
Terrain: Low hills and fells with a few rocky outcrops
Surface: Good forest roads with moderate climbs and excellent descents
(Darling How has some boggy sections)
Start Point Grid Reference: 208245, Whinlatter Visitor Centre
Maps: O.S. The English Lakes 1:25 000 NW sheet, Forestry Commission
Guide Map (available from the Visitor Centre)

Overleaf right: Overlooking Spout Force in the Thornthwaite Forest.

To the west of Keswick is the Whinlatter Pass which connects Braithwaite with Lorton Vale and climbs to a height of 1075ft. Straddling the pass is the Thornthwaite Forest, Britain's oldest national forest - established by the Forestry Commission in 1919. Kindly, the commission has allowed mountain bikers access to Thornthwaite Forest on tracks that are not rights of way, on the condition that they avoid foresting operations - check at the Visitor Centre. The plantations north of the pass are the most extensive in Thornthwaite Forest and cover the fells of Graystones, Whinlatter and Lord's Seat, whilst to the south they extend onto the fells of Grisedale Pike. The route open to mountain bikers starts at the Visitor Centre and works its way around Whinlatter over classic forest roads. At no point is the going difficult and there are plenty of viewpoints, location points and signs making it an ideal venue for beginners. For those wishing to develop skills and techniques Darling How Plantation is the place; quiet and off the beaten track there are climbs and obstacles to everybody's taste.

Route Description

The route starts behind the Visitor Centre and zig-zags up hill in long easy sections; firstly N to location point 1; turns L and backtracks S to Horsebox Crossroads; then turns R and heads N again - follow it as it swings W to a junction at Tarbarrel Moss. Continue W straight across the junction up a short climb to the crest of a hill. You are now poised at the top of a $2\frac{1}{2}$m descent which heads N then W and follows the course of Aiken Beck - watch your speed on this section as there may be walkers in the middle of the track. If you feel like some bumps and bruises and a lot of fun head for Darling How, which can be reached by crossing Aiken Beck at location point 28 (2m from the top of the descent). If not it is worth making a short detour to have a look at Spout Force, then continue down to the Whinlatter Pass road.

To return to the Visitor Centre head up the pass for 1m until it is possible to turn R at a car park and pick up a forest track that runs parallel with the road on the S side. Follow this track as it climbs easily above the top of the pass and then drops sharply back to the road at the Comb Bridge. All that remains now is a short climb W up the road to the Visitor Centre.

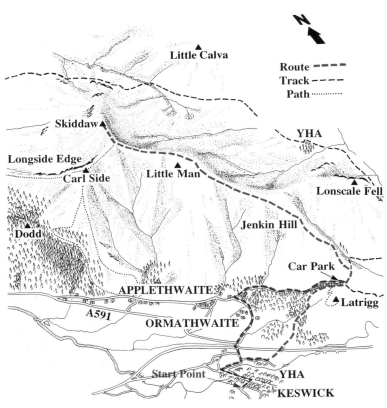

N

Route ----
Track ----
Path ········

Little Calva

Skiddaw

YHA

Longside Edge

Carl Side

Little Man

Lonscale Fell

Dodd

Jenkin Hill

Car Park

APPLETHWAITE

Latrigg

A591

ORMATHWAITE

Start Point

YHA

KESWICK

Skiddaw

Grade: Very Difficult - **Time:** 2½ Hours - **Height Gain:** 2800ft
Distance: 10½ Miles - 6½ off road, 4 on road
Terrain: High exposed mountain and fells
Surface: Steep road, smooth steep fell side, rocky summit ridge, rutted bridleway
Start Point Grid Reference: 266233, Keswick
Maps: O.S. The English Lakes 1:25 000 NW sheet

Wherever you are in Keswick there is no ignoring Skiddaw - smooth slopes and angular buttresses form a conical mass that dominates the northern sky-line. It does not take two glances to realise that the geology of Skiddaw is different to that of its southern neighbours. The slates and shales of which it is formed erode uniformly leaving few' features save a thin covering of scree and the huge gullies cut by the action of becks. This uniform terrain offers the mountain biker easy but exciting going. Luckily Skiddaw is serviced by a bridleway from the car park at Latrigg which reaches the summit via a steep climb up Jenkin Hill.

Route Description

Although there is a bridleway from Briar Rigg on the outskirts of Keswick to the Latrigg car park, it is probably easier to take the road, and save the bridleway for the return descent. From the centre of Keswick take the A5271 past the pencil works, turn R at the junction and follow it up to the big roundabout on the A66. Go straight across the roundabout, join the A591 and immediately turn right for Applethwaite and Ormathwaite. Follow this road for 1m and turn R at a junction just past the entrance to the Underscar Hotel. Latrigg car park is reached after one very steep mile.

From the far end of the car park follow the bridleway along a fence until it splits at a gate. Take the left fork which passes over a grassy knoll with a monument on top and arrives at the foot of a steep climb. The section ahead is the steepest part of the ascent and will require some determined carrying; it climbs directly up the fell side to Jenkin Hill and being popular presents no route finding problems. After ½m the track swings round to the NW, and the angle relents somewhat making riding possible. Continue easily across the col near Jenkin Hill through a gate and around the back of Little Man to another gate. One last steep section leads to the summit ridge which is followed N for ¼m over rocky but level going to the summit. There are shelters and a trig point at the summit but of most interest is the viewpointer mounted on a circular cairn.

The descent returns along the same route to the car park and, is without doubt the easiest and fastest descent from above 3000ft in England and Wales! This route is very popular with walkers and has sheep grazing on it - so pay due consideration and moderate your speed accordingly. To continue back to Keswick off road, follow the bridleway (Cumbria Way) which skirts SW around Latrigg and crosses the bridge over the A66. Generally this track is quite fast, but the steeper rutted middle section could cause the odd mishap. After crossing a bridge over the A66 the track joins the road at Briar Rigg; turn R and follow the road until it joins the A5271.

Overleaf left: Derwent Water from Jenkin Hill, Skiddaw.

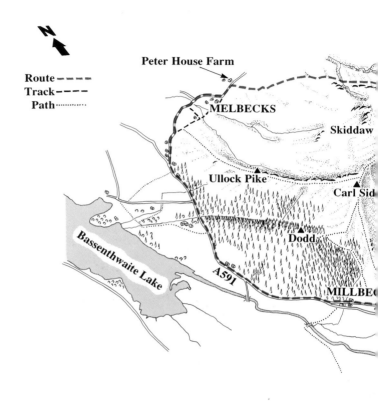

Tour of Skiddaw

Grade: Difficult - Time: 4 hours - Height Gain: 1230ft
Distance: 14 Miles - 7 off road, 7 on road
Terrain: Open moorland and low fells
Surface: Stony, well graded bridleways and tracks
Start Point Grid Reference: 281253, Latrigg car park
Maps: O.S. The English Lakes 1:25 000 NW sheet, O.S. Pathfinder 576
Caldbeck NY 23/33 sheet

Overleaf right: Looking to Longside Edge from Skiddaw.

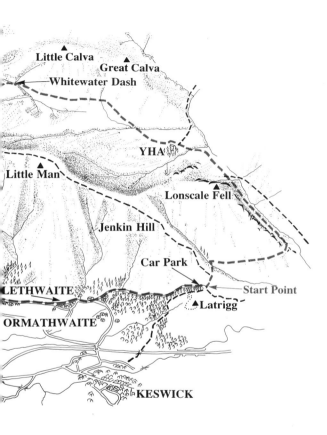

North of Skiddaw lies an area of high moors and rolling hills, bleak and lonely - these fells do not attract the crowds as their southern neighbours do. Great sweeps of open fells dominate the landscape relieved only by becks. Penetrating this wilderness is a bridleway that skirts the eastern flanks of Lonscale Fell and then heads north west over Burnt Horse and around the back of Skiddaw. By starting at Latrigg and following this bridleway it is possible to make a complete tour of Skiddaw over good tracks with only a moderate height gain and take in some spectacular scenery.

Route Description

From the car park at Latrigg follow the bridleway for Skiddaw next to a fence and wall until it splits at a gate. Take the R branch which crosses Whit Beck in a sheltered ravine and then traverses Lonscale Fell. Until this point the going has been easy but this all changes once Lonscale Crags are rounded. The once broad track narrows to a terrace high amongst the crags providing some testing riding! The terrace contours the steep slope for over a mile, and is followed until it meets another bridleway from Blease Fell. Continue N across the moor slowly gaining height until after ½m Burnt Horse is reached. At this point the route heads NW, crossing a beck and peat hags (boggy) with a final short climb up to Skiddaw House. Being the highest point on the route and with dominating views of three watersheds, Skiddaw House is an ideal resting place - originally a shepherds dwelling it is now run as a Youth Hostel (change from The English Lakes NW to the Pathfinder 576 Caldbeck NY 23/33 O.S. map).

From Skiddaw House run two other bridleways one NE towards Carrock Fell and Mosedale; the other a service track runs NW across the flanks of Great Calva and Little Calva - follow this easily to a ford and foot bridge. The track climbs steadily for ½m until a beck is crossed, and then descends, giving ½m freewheeling to a hairpin bend and bridge. Downstream of the bridge in a gorge is the Whitewater Dash waterfall - well worth a look especially after heavy rainfall. The track continues to descend steeply at first, and can clearly be seen contouring below the spectacular Dead Crags, which drop abruptly from Bakestall. Exciting riding leads to the road at Peter House Farm; turn left and follow it for 2m through Melbecks and join the A591. Head S towards Keswick for 3m and then take the Millbeck and Applethwaite road which after another 3m and a very steep climb leads back to the car park at Latrigg.

The excellent access track that descends across the NE flank of Skiddaw

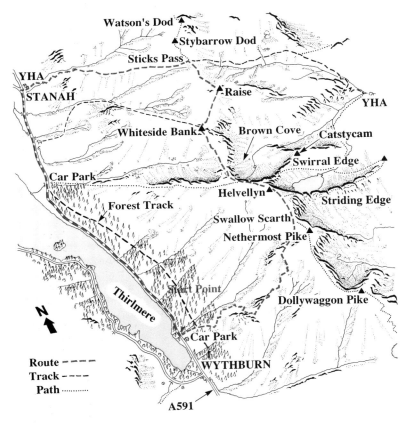

Helvellyn West

Grade: Severe - **Time:** 4 Hours - **Height Gain:** 2972ft
Distance: 9½ Miles - 8 off road, 1½ on road
Terrain: High mountain ridge
Surface: Steep rocky ascent, broad open fell tops and a narrow ridge encountered in descent
Start Point Grid Reference: 324137, Wythburn
Map: O.S The English Lakes 1:25 000 NE sheet

Helvellyn is the highest point on a range of fells which run in a north-south direction, and take the appearance of a great whale back. To the west they border Thirlmere with steep open fells, forested to the 1700ft contour. Fast flowing becks provide the only real distraction amongst this uniform landscape. To the east the Helvellyn range is a different story; steep-sided dales with alpine-type corries and ridges at their heads descend to the shores of Ullswater, forming a natural boundary to the range. Features like Striding Edge and Swirral Edge are an attraction for walkers all year round, but for climbers the main attractions are the consistent snow and ice conditions found in the winter months. From Nethermost Pike to Sticks Pass the main summit ridge does not drop below the 2500ft contour, and is characterised by rocky but level ground, interspersed with short steep descents to cols and bounded by precipices to the E. The summit of Helvellyn is so level that in 1926 Bert Hinkeler landed a light aircraft; the spot now marked by a stone tablet, one of the many man-made objects that litter the summit.

Route Description

From the car park in the disused quarry at Wythburn follow the old pony-track through the forest on the right-hand side of Comb Gill. This track leads in a series of zig-zags to Swallow Scarth and then on to Helvellyn; it is steep, loose, and because you will mostly need to carry your bike, it is hard work! The advantages are many; easy navigation, wonderful views down Thirlmere and best of all the wind rush as you stand on the very edge of the crags at Swallow Scarth, taking in the wild scenery below. The route now joins the main ridge track; follow this in a N direction; ½m of easy riding leads directly to the summit and its attendant shelter. Helvellyn is renowned for its sunrise views, but it is an impressive place to be at any time of the day, and therefore you will be very lucky to have it to yourself.

Cross the summit plateau in a NW direction, passing the path which descends to Swirral Edge (marked by a cairn) and then make for the cairn of Lower Man. In poor visibility the route to Lower Man is very confusing - from the trig point on Helvellyn follow a bearing of 295° (grid) for 500yds then 340° for 100yds to the cairn. From Lower Man the route follows a steep narrow ridge down to the col above Brown Cove. This ridge is the crux of the whole route and can be very exciting; a fall here could have serious consequences - great care should be taken. If in doubt get off and walk! Continue N across the col and ascend the slopes of Whiteside Bank. The fells to the E become less steep and the track along the ridge less distinct so when leaving Whiteside Bank make sure you take the right route, which is to the NE. The going is easy over grass and small loose stones, with the occasional bigger rock to get you out of the saddle. The ascent to Raise is not too steep but will quicken your breathing enough to make you appreciate a rest on top.

From Raise drop down to Sticks Pass then descend W across a smooth grassy fell side. At this point there are numerous vague paths; you should stay on the north side of Sticks Gill and cross the ridge above it. The path then becomes more distinct and heads down the fell to the N. As the path reaches the slopes above Stanah Gill it steepens and starts to zig-zag providing fast and furious fun. At Stanah the A591 Ambleside to Keswick road is reached; follow this for 3½m back to the Wythburn car park.

The summit of Helvellyn
from the Gough Memorial

At the col below the crux section of Helvellyn West

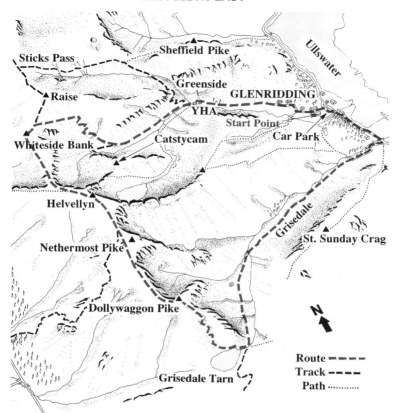

Helvellyn East

Grade: Severe - Time: 4$\frac{1}{2}$ Hours - Height Gain: 3131ft
Distance: 13 Miles - 10 off road, 3 on road
Terrain: High mountain ridge
Surface: Well graded packhorse trail, smooth summit ridge with one difficult climb up a narrow rocky section, steep loose descent and a rocky valley track
Start Point Grid Reference: 386170, Glenridding
Map: O.S. The English Lakes 1:25 000 NE sheet

Viewed from Glenridding or Patterdale the eastern side of Helvellyn hardly looks like perfect mountain bike country - craggy corries and ridges present a formidable barrier which is only easily breached on foot by scrambling up either Striding Edge or Swirral Edge. To gain access with mountain bikes you need to look at each end of the range. To the north from Glenridding a bridleway works its way past Greenside mines and gains the main ridge by climbing Keppel Cove in a clever series of zig-zags; and to the south from Patterdale a good track along Grisedale gains the ridge via the slopes above Grisedale Tarn. Once the ridge is gained excellent riding can be had on the range's broad summit slopes. In descent the route south from the summit of Helvellyn is by far the best option - a long run with fine situations and many difficult but mostly rideable obstacles.

Route Description

The route to Keppel Cove starts at the disused mining complex at Greenside which is reached from Glenridding by taking the minor road off the A592 opposite the Ullswater Hotel. Go straight through the mine complex and follow a good track as it gradually climbs SW (don't cross Glenridding Beck). After 1m take the path off to the R (cairn) that climbs through a series of zig-zags then traverses W high above Keppel Cove. The traverse provides pleasant riding to a col on the main ridge below Whiteside Bank. Ascend Whiteside Bank and pass S straight over the summit to make a fast easy descent down to the col below Lower Man. Continue S and climb the steep rocky ridge to Lower Man and gain the long summit plateau of Helvellyn. Gentle grassy slopes fall away to the W but to the E a great sweep of crags and scree drop unabated to Red Tarn. Easily but carefully follow the path on the plateau above the E face past the trig point to the low outcrop of rocks that mark the summit (a useful walled shelter is situated on the SE side).

From the summit head S and descend to Swallow Scarth; ignore the track that branches R and continue S with a short climb over Nethermost Pike. The excellent riding continues past Dollywagon Pike to the start of the steep descent to Grisedale Tarn. The track down to the tarn does zig-zag but parts of it are very steep and very loose - a complete descent in the saddle without skidding or falling off would be quite an achievement. From Grisedale Tarn head NE below Tarn Crag (don't cross the outlet beck) on a rocky track to the head of Grisedale. Continue along the track over a series of rock steps and down an awkward rutted section to Ruthwaite Lodge. After the Lodge the track relents a little in difficulty until a good track can be reached by crossing Grisedale Beck at a ford and foot bridge. Continue easily along Grisedale for 2m to join the access road which is followed back to the A592 at Patterdale. Turn L and take the main road by Ullswater back to Glenridding.

The summit of Helvellyn

Nearing Whiteside Bank, Helvellyn with Catstycam in the distance

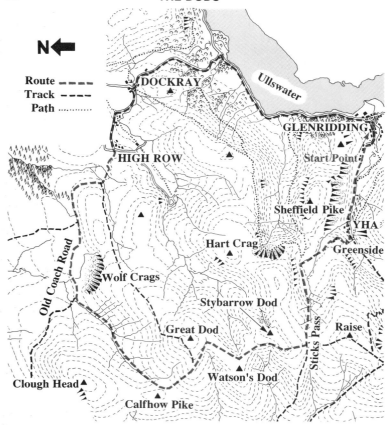

The Dods

Grade: Very Difficult - **Time:** 5 Hours - **Height Gain:** 2555ft
Distance: 13½ Miles - 8½ off road, 5 on road
Terrain: High rounded mountains
Surface: Mining road, steep but well graded packhorse track, smooth grassy ridge, smooth but boggy valley, well graded coach road.
Start Point Grid Reference: 386170, Glenridding
Map: O.S. The English Lake District 1:25 000 NE sheet

North of Sticks Pass the character of the long Helvellyn range changes dramatically. The smooth grassy slopes and featureless summits of Stybarrow Dod, Watson's Dod and Great Dod contrast with the rocky corries and ridges of Helvellyn. Not that popular with walkers, the plateau formed by the Dods is quiet and offers mountain bikers a mountain traverse with riding terrain second to none. Like the rest of the Helvellyn range the Dods have an excellent net-work of bridleways which can be joined at Sticks Pass in the S or by the Old Coach Road to the N. Both routes are long hard slogs in ascent but Sticks Pass is probably the better as it is well graded and dry. In poor visibility navigation on the ridge could be tricky as the start of the descent route to the Old Coach Road is not that clear.

Route Description

The route to Sticks Pass starts at the disused lead mining complex at Greenside which is reached from Glenridding by taking the minor road off the A592 opposite the Ullswater Hotel. The road heads W for 1½m pleasantly following above Glenridding Beck. Past the YHA and the old mine buildings the Sticks Pass track zig-zags through the spoil heaps and then zig-zags up and around Stang End on well graded terraces. Continue round Stang End until Sticks Gill can be crossed at the bridge below an old dam. Head NW a short distance across fine gravel and stones then follow the path as it makes a rising traverse W across the lower slopes of Stybarrow Dod. The traverse is easy at first and can be ridden but as it climbs towards Sticks Pass the gradient steepens considerably forcing a carry and only easing as the ridge is gained.

S from Sticks Pass is Raise and the main bulk of the Helvellyn range; the route lies to the N with a steep climb to Stybarrow Dod. The climb is smooth and just about rideable - a real muscle buster! From Stybarrow Dodd (not the trig point) easy riding leads NW for ¾m to Watson's Dod with some overall height loss. Level riding NE then a short pull leads to the high point of the route Great Dod at 2807ft.

From Great Dod a bridleway can be taken that descends NE across Matterdale and joins the Old Coach Road but this cuts off a long interesting section of the return leg. Better to take the fast descent NW to the lowest part of the col below Calfhow Pike; then head down the valley on the E side of the ridge to Mariel Bridge on the Old Coach Road. This descent is entertaining being bumpy on the ridge and boggy in the valley - worth having a camera ready to catch those thrills and spills! Once the Old Coach Road is reached, follow it E to a fast descent to the road head at High Row. A 2½m freewheel leads R through a T-junction at Dockray then down to another T-junction on the A592 by the side of Ullswater. Turn R and follow the road back to Glenridding.

The steep climb up Stang End

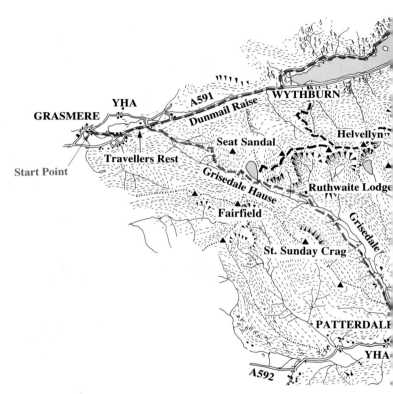

Tour of Helvellyn

Grade: Severe - Time: 6½ Hours - Height Gain: 2894ft
Distance: 28 Miles - 10 off road, 18 on road
Terrain: High mountain and moorland passes
**Surface: Steep rocky packhorse road, easy well graded coach road and
busy roads**
Start Point Grid Reference: 337075, Grasmere (The English Lakes SE sheet)
Maps: O.S. The English Lakes 1:25 000 SE, NE and NW sheets

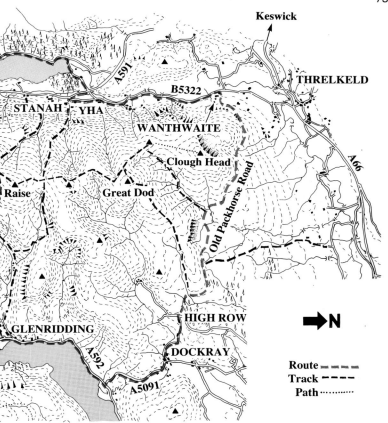

Keswick

THRELKELD

A591   B5322

STANAH   YHA

WANTHWAITE

Clough Head

Old Packhorse Road

Raise   Great Dod

A66

HIGH ROW

➡N

GLENRIDDING

A592

DOCKRAY

A5091

Route ― ― ―
Track ‐ ‐ ‐ ‐
Path ·············

For those with a thirst for distance, a tour of Helvellyn is a must. A route can be made right around the range that makes use of the old coach road to the north and old pack horse road to the south, providing a mountain bike route that has something for everybody. Steep technical sections, fast rough tracks and plenty of road work combine with the ever changing mountain scenery to give a long but rewarding day out. By starting with an ascent of the old packhorse road from Grasmere the hard technical work can be completed while you are still fresh and before fatigue sets in.

Route Description

Out of Grasmere join the A591 and follow it N until it is possible to turn R onto the old packhorse road just after a bridge 250yds past the Travellers Rest Inn. Although well graded the old packhorse road is none the less very steep climbing straight up Seat Sandal along the course of Little Tongue Gill and only relenting as it contours E then NE to make a final zig-zag up to Grisedale Hause. Follow the track over the Hause and down to Grisedale Tarn. Cross the outlet beck and head NE below Tarn Crag on a rocky track to the head of Grisedale. Continue along the track over a series of rock steps and down an awkward rutted section to Ruthwaite Lodge. After the Lodge the track relents a little until a good track can be reached by crossing Grisedale Beck at a ford and foot bridge. Continue easily along Grisedale for 2m to join the access road which is followed down to the A592 at Patterdale.

From Patterdale take the A592 N for 3m through Glenridding and along the shores of Ullswater until a L turn can be made onto the A5091. Follow the A5091 for 1½m as it climbs to Dockray. At Dockray turn L and take the minor road through to High Row where the Old Coach Road can be joined.

The Old Coach Road maintains a consistent height as it skirts Matterdale Common and Clough Head at the northern end of the the Helvellyn range giving excellent riding. Start along the Old Coach Road from the gate opposite the top of the minor road from Dockray and follow it W for 4½m. Generally the going is easy but there are some boggy sections and a couple of climbs. The last 2m section down to the B5322 at Wanthwaite is steep and very fast.

From Wanthwaite take the B5322 S down St. John's in the Vale to Stanah and a junction with the A591. The A591 can be taken straight back to Grasmere but it's quieter and more interesting to take the minor road around the back of Thirlmere. Turn R onto the A591 and backtrack N for ½m to pick up the lake road at the first L. The Lake road is followed S for 5m to rejoin the A591 at Wythburn. Turn R and head S as the road climbs to Dunmail Raise. The pull up Dunmail Raise is rewarded by a 3m freewheel back to Grasmere.

Descending into Grisedale on the Tour of Helvellyn

HIGH STREET

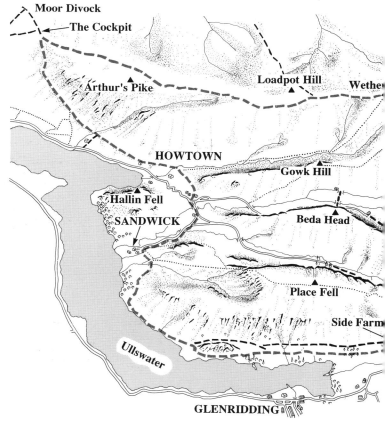

High Street

Grade: Severe - Time: 6 Hours - Height gain: 3500ft
Distance: 22 Miles - 18½ off road, 3½ on road
Terrain: Steep valleys and a long mountain ridge
Surface: Well graded access track, smooth grassy ridge and a rocky bridle-way
Start Point Grid reference: 410131, Hartsop
Maps: O.S. English Lakes 1:25 000 NE sheet

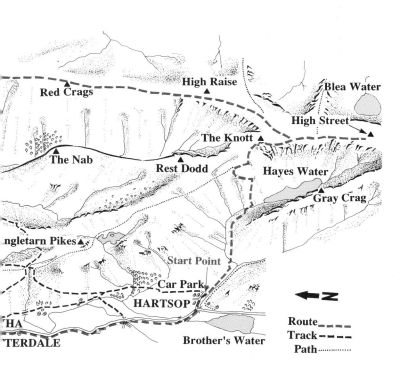

To be able to maintain height for a considerable distance over easy, but mountainous terrain is a rare and desirable experience for mountain bikers, an experience provided by the High Street range of fells. The main ridge runs north to south forming a watershed between Martindale and Patterdale in the west and Mardale (Haweswater) in the east. The route starts by attaining Racecourse Hill at 2719ft via Hayes Water and The Knott; then heads north along the course of an old Roman road gradually descending for 5m until Loadpot Hill is reached - at no point dropping below the 2000ft contour. On descending from the tops, the return journey is made along a bridleway that skirts the shores of Ullswater, a particularly pleasant place to be, especially in the evening with the Helvellyn range and Ullswater catching the sun's last rays.

Route Description.

From Hartsop take the well graded access track that crosses then follows Hayeswater Gill on the R bank to a ford 200yds down stream of the Water Board dam at Hayes Water (if you don't fancy wet feet there is a bridge just below the dam). Take the zig-zags that climb E up to The Knott and join the path from Angle Tarn before the last pull around the summit. From the col behind The Knott ride easily S for 1m along High Street to Racecourse Hill (trig point slightly off the track); the track is clear and should be stuck to especially in mist as there are crags to the W and E. Return the same way till the track splits; the L fork goes back to The Knott; take the R fork which climbs NE. After a short descent, another climb leads to High Raise and the start of a long downhill run along the course of a Roman Road; follow it as it heads roughly N for 6m. Most of this leg is fast easy cycling, but there are some short pulls up to the summits of Red Crag, Wether Hill and Loadpot Hill (at some points the track is not clear on the ground, but if you stick to the crest of the ridge you cannot go far wrong). A very fast grassy slope leads to a junction at the Cockpit; the route turns sharp L, backtracks, and heads SW down a terrace for 3m to Howtown and the shores of Ullswater.

Before you drop into Howtown continue along the track as it makes a rising traverse around the Coombs for 1m to join the road below Hallin Fell - thus maintaining height and avoiding the steep zig-zags on the road. Follow the road round to Sandwick where a bridleway along the shores of Ullswater can be picked up; follow it as it works its way across the many crags and becks above the lake to Side Farm where the A592 can be joined and followed S to Hartsop.

Starting the ascent to High Street — Gray Crag in the distance

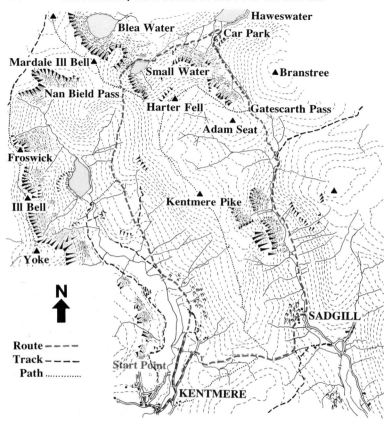

Kentmere, Longsleddale and Mardale

Grade: Severe - Time: 5½ Hours - Height Gain: 3025ft
Distance: 11½ Miles - 10 off road, 1½ on road
Terrain: High mountain passes
Surface: Steep well graded packhorse trails, boggy in parts
Start Point Grid Reference: 456041, Kentmere
Maps: O.S. The English Lakes 1:25 000 SE sheet

Kentmere, Longsleddale and Mardale, are linked by a series of three high level passes, the crossing of which makes an excellent mountain bike tour. The three valleys occupy an area in the south east corner of the Lake District National Park. Partly because of their geographical position and partly because of ignorance about their qualities, they are less frequented than the Lake District's more central valleys. Each valley has its own special feel - Kentmere a busy working community with farms and houses tucked beneath crags and trees, Mardale a flooded valley with its community long gone and Longsleddale a sleepy backwater. The only really difficult section on the three passes is the north side of Nan Bield Pass above Small Water which is best taken in ascent; thus forcing an anti-clockwise direction for the tour.

Route Description

From Kentmere Church head S back down the road and cross Low Bridge then turn sharp L and climb the road to Green Quarter. Turn L again and follow the road for 300yds to a fork. Take the R branch for ½m to a R turn onto a track. Follow the track as it steadily climbs past Stile End and works its way across the ridge and down a fast descent to Sadgill in Longsleddale.

From Sadgill turn L over the bridge and follow the track N up the valley. Follow the track easily for the first 2m. As the head of Longsleddale is reached, the track steepens and makes a steady climb to a flat boggy confluence of becks below Adam Seat. After crossing the River Sprint continue NW and along the main track as it climbs steeply at first through a series of newly constructed zig-zags. As the top of Gatescarth Pass is approached the gradient eases and the surface deteriorates into a boggy mass caused by the destructive action of motorbikes - take care not to add to this erosion and tread warily. From the top of Gatescarth Pass a wonderfully graded track desends NW; follow it for 1m to the car park at the head of Haweswater.

To gain the top of Nan Bield Pass a climb of 1150ft is required. The climb is a hard slog but benefits from passing through some spectacularly wild mountain scenery especially above Small Water. Start by backtracking from the car park and take the R branch as the track forks; follow as it climbs the fell SW to Small Water. Continue around the N side of Small Water and make a steep climb up the zig-zags to the top of Nan Bield Pass. The top of Nan Bield Pass is the start of a classic 4m descent; just the right balance between distance and gradient. The crux of the descent is a steep series of zig-zags directly below the top of the Pass - very testing especially if it is windy! After the zig-zags, continue easily S as the track traverses the slopes above Kentmere Reservoir and crosses the boggy ground above Tongue

Scar. Pass Tongue Scar on the L and continue down on a good track by the river. Climb slightly then descend again past Overend Farm and take the lower track back towards Green Quarter turning R down the lane taken at the start of the route, back to Kentmere.

The cairn at Nan Bield Pass

The Kentmere side of Nan Bield Pass

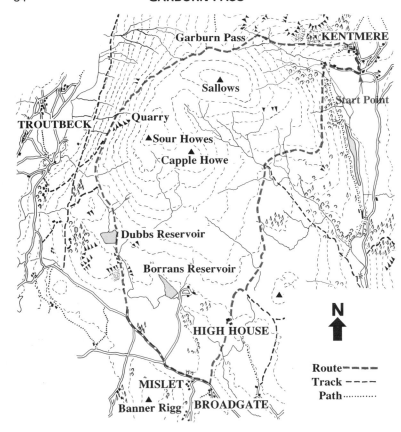

Garburn Pass

Grade: Moderate - Time: 2½ Hours - Height Gain: 1270ft
Distance: 9 Miles - 7½ off road, 1½ on road
Terrain: Hills and low fells
Surface: Wide well graded drove road rough in parts, narrow road, farm tracks and a vague bridleway
Start Point Grid Reference: 456041, Kentmere
Map: O.S. The English Lakes 1:25 000 SE sheet

The old drove roads and packhorse trails that criss-cross the Lakeland fells tend to follow logical well graded courses that offer the line of least resistance over high ground. The Garburn Pass connecting Kentmere and Troutbeck is a classic example of this sort of route; the traversing of which makes an exciting mountain bike ride. A steep climb to the top of the pass from Kentmere gives quick access to a wonderful downhill cruise high above Troutbeck. The return leg is no less interesting with a brief section on the road and the rest on an easy bridleway.

Route Description

The Garburn Pass starts in Kentmere at a cluster of houses ¼m up the road from the church. Head up the lane past Badger Rock (large boulder in the field on the R) and then continue W along the track for 1m as it steepens and climbs over boulders and rock steps to the top of the pass. Continue easily over the top and follow the track as it swings round to the SW. The track becomes rougher as it steepens with some nasty ruts that will put the unwary on the deck. Pass under the old quarry and take the L fork at a junction in front of a stand of trees. Make a short climb then continue down the track passing Dubbs Reservoir to the road. Turn L and follow the road for 1m to a farm gate on the L (entrance to High House Farm). Head up the farm drive and pass through the farm to pick up a bridleway heading N. Take the bridleway as it climbs up a lane then veers E to a junction. Turn sharp L and head N again along a wall for 1m to the corner of a field which is crossed to a ford (bridleway is vague on the ground). After the ford the bridleway becomes a more distinct track and is followed as it skirts the steep fell side above the trees. A final steep run leads down to Kentmere Hall Farm after which a driveway is followed back to Kentmere church.

Overleaf left: On the Kentmere side of the Garburn Pass.

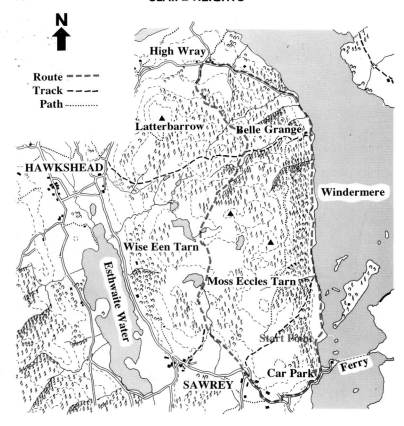

N

Route ----
Track ----
Path ....

High Wray

Latterbarrow ▲

Belle Grange

HAWKSHEAD

Windermere

Wise Een Tarn ▲

▲

Moss Eccles Tarn

Esthwaite Water

Start Point

Car Park Ferry

SAWREY

Claife Heights

Grade: Easy - Time: 1½ Hours - Height Gain: 620ft
Distance 7½ Miles - 5 off road, 2½ on road
Terrain: Low wooded hills
Surface: Good tracks but muddy in parts
Start Point Grid Reference: 388954, car park near Ferry House, Lake Windermere
Map: O.S. The English Lakes 1:25 000 SE sheet

Overleaf right: The Windermere ferry – Claife Heights beyond.

Claife Heights, an area of low fells lying west of Lake Windermere, is an excellent venue for those new to mountain biking. Its tree-covered slopes are bisected by bridleways and tracks that are at no point difficult, but do provide great sport with climbs, short fast descents, fords, and a profusion of muddy pools. The area can be easily reached by car but (if it is running) the ferry from Bowness is always worth taking.

Route Description

From the car park near the Ferry House follow the B5285 to Far Sawrey past the Sawrey Hotel and turn R (bridleway) into a lane which leads into Claife Heights. The bridleway winds its way N for 3½m through Claife Heights, first past Moss Eccles Tarn, then by Wise Een Tarn and eventually drops down to High Wray. Navigation can be tricky because of the number of tracks and paths about, but as long as you head roughly N, you should not encounter too many problems.

From the junction at High Wray, follow the road past Balla Wray to the car park at Red Nab and then on round the track above the lake to Belle Grange. To return to the Ferry House, simply follow the track by the lake for 2½m. Claife Heights is a popular area with walkers and horse riders - so do not forget they have right of way over mountain bikes.

BANISHEAD MOOR

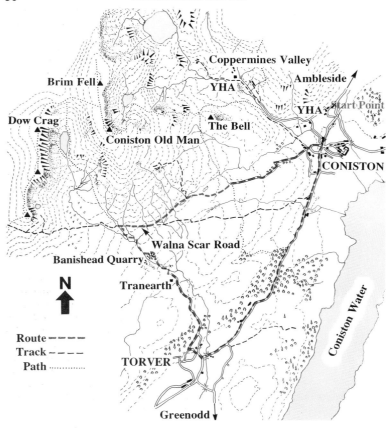

Banishead Moor

Grade: Moderate - Time: 1½ Hours - Height Gain: 1000ft
Distance: 5 Miles - 3 off road, 2 on road
Terrain: Moorland and low fells
Surface: Tracks and quarry roads
Start Point Grid Reference: 302976, Coniston
Map: O.S. The English Lakes 1:25 000 SW sheet

Mining and quarrying have been the life blood of Coniston for centuries, scarring the surrounding hills with holes and spoil heaps. Through all this exploitation the peaks have retained their powerful presence, offering much to those who spend time in this corner of Lakeland, even amongst man's despoilation. By taking advantage of the Walna Scar Road (an old packhorse route) and old and quarrying tracks, it is possible to experience the feel of a true mountain bike tour. The short duration of this route, easy navigation and good tracks make it ideally suited as an introduction for beginners or as an evening or bad weather alternative for the more experienced mountain biker.

Route Description

From the centre of Coniston take the minor road to the Sun Hotel; follow it past the hotel round a bend to the foot of a very steep hill; and the start of the Walna Scar Road. Climb the hill which eases after ¼m and continue along the road to the fell gate - the end of the metalled surface. Above the fell gate, follow the road/track W as it gradually rises passing the new quarry road and Boo Tarn. Continue as it steepens through two rock gates (which make interesting test-pieces for your riding skill) until a large cairn is reached.

From the cairn a bridleway descends SE; follow it to Banishead quarry. The bridleway is vague at first and steep; you should stay to the left of Torver Beck, crossing other smaller tributaries until you reach the quarry which is quite large and filled with water - care should be taken exploring around the quarry especially near the waterfall. Below the main quarry the route becomes more defined and has many obstacles - a good place to test skills required in descending steep terrain or manoeuvering over larger rocks on the harder routes. Past Banishead the route follows a meandering old lane which is over-grown and muddy but pleasant. A final bone-shaking dash past some cottages and a sharp left-hander leads to the main road at Torver, which is then followed back to Coniston.

N.B. After descending through Banishead Quarry, cross Torver Beck and stay on the R or SW side – this is a bridleway: the L or NE side is a footpath and out-of-bounds to cyclists.

Overleaf left: Descent through the quarries at Tranearth, Banishead.

THE WALNA SCAR ROAD

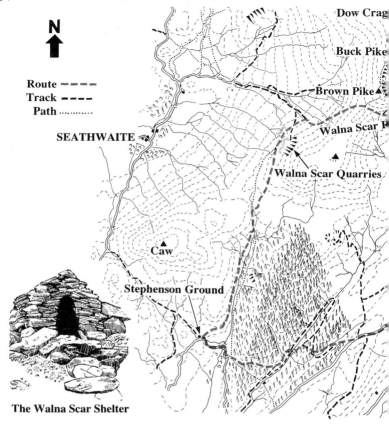

N

Route -- -- --
Track - - - -
Path ....

Dow Crag
Buck Pike
Brown Pike ▲
Walna Scar R
SEATHWAITE
Walna Scar Quarries
▲ **Caw**
Stephenson Ground

The Walna Scar Shelter

The Walna Scar Road

Grade: Difficult - Time: 4-4$\frac{1}{2}$ Hours - Height Gain: 1970ft
Distance: 11$\frac{1}{2}$ Miles - 6 off road, 5$\frac{1}{2}$ on road
Terrain: High mountain pass
Surface: Old packhorse road with generally good going but boggy in parts
and forest tracks
Start Point Grid Reference: 303977, Coniston
Map: O.S. The English Lakes 1:25 000 SW sheet

Overleaf right: Cove Bridge, Walna Scar road, Dow Crag beyond.

West of Coniston and the Old Man is a high ridge of fells extending south west from Dow Crag to the Walna Scar and then on down to the coast at Duddon Bridge. Only at the Walna Scar does the ridge drop below the 2000ft contour, at which point it is crossed by an old packhorse road. The road connects Seathwaite in the isolated Duddon valley with Coniston and was at one time a busy route. With the opening up of other passes to traffic, and the arrival of the now disused railway line to Coniston, the Walna Scar Road fell from favour. The ravages of weather and lack of maintenance have taken a toll on the "Road", but its course can still easily be followed. In fact for mountain bikers its present state is perfect; plenty of tricky but rideable sections both up and downhill - a challenge to even the most capable of riders.

Route Description

From the centre of Coniston take the minor road to the Sun Hotel; follow it past the hotel round a bend to the foot of a very steep hill. Climb the hill which eases after ¼m and continue along it to the fell gate - the end of the metalled surface. Three tracks lead from the fell gate; R is the tourist route up the Old Man, L is a path down to Bleathwaite and straight ahead (SW) is the Walna Scar Road - follow it easily as it crosses rough moorland below the Old Man. After ½m a quarry track leads off steeply to the R; ignore it and continue straight ahead past Boo Tarn and through a couple of tricky rock gates. Follow the track past a large cairn to Cove Bridge. To the N lies the Cove and Dow Crag. Continue W towards the ridge easily at first until the gradient steepens through a series of rock cuttings and zig-zags, after which the route eases as a small shelter is passed and the crest is reached.

The descent on the Duddon side skirts SW along the steep, grassy slopes of Walna Scar for ½m, then round a long bend which takes it NW straight down the fell side. Just after the bend the route takes a L turn at a gate and leaves the Walna Scar Road. Follow the track below the Walna Scar quarries S for 1m across boggy moorland which can be quite difficult, as the track's true course is not clear on the ground, and cross a beck (upper reaches of the River Lickle) to a good track on the R bank. Excellent riding for 1½m leads to a road at Stephenson Ground Farm. Turn L and recross the River Lickle at Water Yeat Bridge; continue along the road for a short distance and then turn L into the forest. A short pull leads to a junction; turn R and backtrack 100yds down the forest track till it is possible to turn L into the trees. This is supposedly the start of a bridleway, but on the ground it is very vague. Head roughly SE through the trees and over a low ridge until you meet another forest track; turn L and follow it NE for ¼m and then down to cross Appletree Worth Beck at a bridge. On the other side, the track leads to a junction; turn R and then follow it as it climbs another low ridge out of the forest to join a road. Turn L and follow down a steep fast hill to the A593 which is taken back to Coniston.

Extra-mural activities on the Walna Scar Road

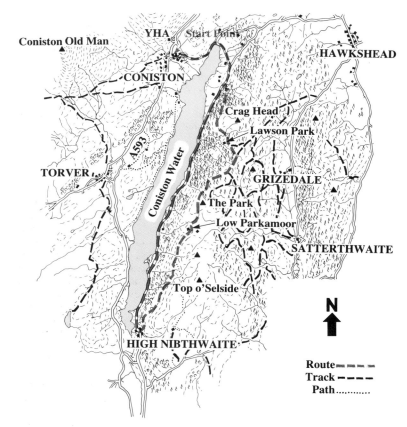

Grizedale Forest and Selside

Grade: Moderate - **Time:** 2-2½ Hours - **Height Gain:** 800ft
Distance: 13½ Miles - 5 off road, 8½ on road
Terrain: Low fells
Surface: Steep bridleway, forestry tracks and roads, open grassy fell with some rock outcrops and a stony access track
Start Point Grid Reference: 303976, Coniston
Map: O.S. The English Lakes 1:25 000 SW sheet

Most of the low fells east of Coniston Water are covered by woodland and forestry plantations. As is usual with forestry operations there is an extensive network of access tracks. Fortunately a series of waymarked and colour coded cycle routes have been opened up by the Forestry Commission along these tracks - which are particularly ideal for beginners (further route information can be obtained from the Forestry Commission at Grizedale).

For those wanting more of a challenge there is also an excellent bridleway in the area, that has an easy ascent and a good descent with lots of tricky terrain in between. The bridleway starts at the north end of Coniston Water and traverses south along the low ridge line formed by Crag Head, The Park and Selside to finish at High Nibthwaite.

Route Description

From the centre of Coniston take the Hawkshead road E for 1m to a junction at the head of Coniston Water. Turn R, and follow the road as it climbs to another junction. Continue past the Hawkshead turning and follow the road for ¼m to the start of a bridleway on the L side of the road at a gateway. Follow the bridleway as it climbs S then SE through woodland for 1m to meet a forestry track near Lawson Park. On the other side of the track the bridleway continues (sign posted to Grizedale). Follow the bridleway as it steepens and climbs SE through dense forest to join another forest road - the track is very boggy but its horrors only last for ¼m. At the forest track turn R and follow it S for ¼m to a L hand bend. At the bend the bridleway leaves the track and continues SE; follow it as it skirts high ground (lying to the E) for ½m to a wall near the summit of The Park.

The bridleway coninues S; follow it amongst the bracken and low outcrops for ¾m to Low Parkamoor an old farm house set in a superb position high above Coniston Water. From Low Parkamoor an excellent access track heads S; follow it as it makes a brief climb then descends for 2¼m right into the centre of High Nibthwaite. From High Nibthwaite turn R and join the road; follow it N for 5 ½m along the side of the lake and back to Coniston.

Overleaf left: The final haul up to Lawson Park, Grizedale Forest.

BLACK COMBE

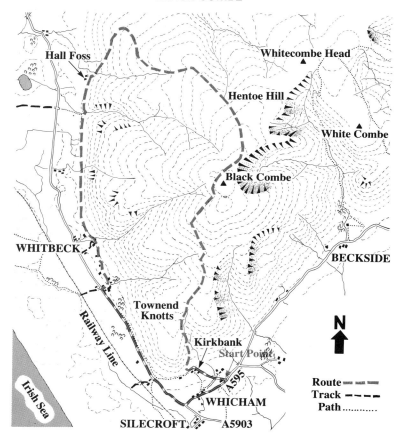

Black Combe

Grade: Difficult - Time: 2½-3 Hours - Height Gain: 1900ft
Distance: 8½ Miles - 7 off road, 1½ on road
Terrain: High coastal fell
Surface: Steep grassy fells and farm tracks
Start Point Grid Reference: 136827, Whicham
Map: O.S. Pathfinder, Broughton in Furness, SD 08/18

Overleaf right: Looking out to sea from Townend Knott on Black Combe.

Situated between sea and mountains the modest peak of Black Combe has some of the best views in the country. Its detached position and moderate height give it a full 360° panorama which, on a clear day, includes part of Scotland and Wales, the Isle of Man, north Lancashire, the western Pennines and of course most of the Lakeland peaks. Black Combe's qualities are not limited to its views; for mountain bikers its rounded profile and excellent tracks offer riding second to none. A bridleway climbs directly to the summit from Whicham and then descends and skirts the northern flank. There are no real navigational problems; and although the climb to the top is a bit of a slog, this route is suitable for both beginners and experts.

Route Description

From the A595 at Whicham take the lane at the side of the church, NW for ¼m a small group of houses. Follow the lane around the back of the houses to a junction with a path. At the junction a bridleway splits off to the R; follow N as it climbs steeply up by the side of Moorgill Beck. After ¾m the track levels at the top of the gill by Townend Knotts. The track continues N and begins to climb; follow it more easily for 1¼m to the summit of Black Combe (shelter and trig point).

From the summit the descent route is to the NE; follow the vague path as it skirts the top of Blackcombe Screes (steep loose crag) and then swings round to the N. Continue N then NW for 1m down the excellent steep grassy slope and past the head of Hentoe Beck to pick up a rough access track. Follow the track W then N and then finally SW across the fell side for 1½m to a ford. Cross the ford and follow the good track on the other side S for 2m through Whitbeck to join the A595 at Townend Hall. Once the A595 is joined, follow it SE for 1½m to a junction; turn L and continue along it a short distance, back to Whicham.

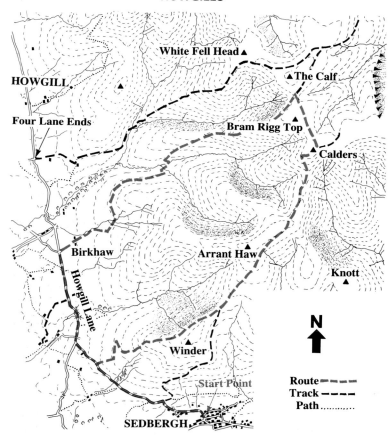

Howgills

Grade: Very Difficult - Time: 3½ Hours - Height Gain: 2425ft
Distance: 10¼ Miles - 7 off road, 3¼ on road
Terrain: High rounded hills
Surface: Narrow road, farm track and steep grassy fells
Start Point Grid Reference: 659922, Sedbergh
Map: O.S. Pathfinder 617 Sedbergh and Baugh Fell, SD 69/79 sheet

Travelling north towards Shap along the Lune valley you can not help but notice an attractive group of hills to the east. These are the Howgills, situated between the Lake District and the Dales, but actually within the boundaries of the Yorkshire Dales National Park. The Howgills are really a range in their own right. For mountain biking they are absolutely ideal; reasonably steep their flanks provide ideal descents, whilst the ridges provide easy riding. The Calf is the highest peak in the group and can be reached in one steep ascent from Howgill Lane via Birkhaw and Bram Rigg. Gaining height by this route allows a long descent back to Sedbergh over Bram Rigg Top, Calders, Arant Haw and Winder.

Route Description

Opposite the church in the centre of Sedbergh is the start of Howgill Lane. Follow it as it climbs up around the back of the town and heads W then NW for 1½m to a junction. Turn R and continue along Howgill Lane for 1m to a crossroads. At the crossroads turn R onto a farm track (bridleway). Follow the track to the farm at Birkhaw. Continue straight through the farm and follow the track as it climbs E then NE to a ford at Eller Mire Beck. Cross the ford and continue along the track as it contours first N then E and then makes a short descent to a ford at Bram Rigg Beck. Up to this point the going has been easy with enjoyable riding, but this is where the work starts. From the other side of the beck the steep uniform ridge of Bram Rigg extends to the E and must be climbed to reach Bram Rigg Top. The height gain up the ridge is nearly 1500ft and is an unremmiting slog, which only eases off near the top. From Bram Rigg Top, The Calf is a short distance to the N across a low col - if you want to visit it you will have to leave your bike at Bram Rigg Top as there is no bridleway between the two summits.

Stretching away to the S from Bram Rigg Top is a long ridge which takes in the rest of the major Howgills summits with only minimal height loss between tops. The route follows this ridge first over Calders which is connected to Bram Rigg Top by a low col. From Calders follow the fence W then S and start the first part of the what must be the best descent in the Dales. The ridge levels and heads SW across Arant Haw then steepens to give a fantastic 2m run down past Winder on the N side and then down Howgill Lane. Turn L onto Howgill Lane and follow it E back to Sedbergh.

Overleaf left: Approaching Winder, the last top on the Howgills route.

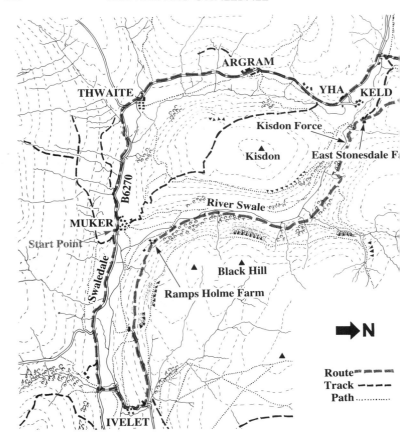

Tan Hill and Swaledale

Grade: Difficult - Time: 4½ Hours - Height Gain: 1220ft
Distance: 17 Miles - 7 off road, 10 on road
Terrain: Valley and exposed moorland
Surface: Steep narrow road, boggy bridleway and farm tracks
Start Point Grid Refernce: 910979, Muker
Maps: O.S. Yorkshire Dales 1:25 000 Northern Area, Landranger 91 & 98
1:50 000

Overleaf right: The Pennine Way S. of the Tan Hill Inn.

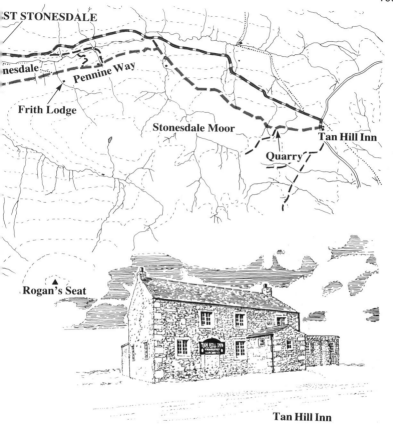

Tan Hill Inn

On the northern boundary of the Yorkshire Dales National Park at the head
of Stonesdale sits the Tan Hill Inn, Britain's highest public house at 1732ft.
Originally it served drovers on their way to market and local coal miners
who worked pits on the surrounding windswept moors. Nowadays its main
trade is from tourists arriving by road and walkers following the Pennine
Way. The Inn is a key landmark on the Pennine Way which runs north east
to Sleigtholme and south to Keld in Swaledale. The section to Keld is a bridleway, which offers easy but interesting mountain biking. It roughly

follows the course of Stonesdale Beck, across the moors, until it joins the River Swale, as it enters a gorge at Kisdon, which it crosses into Keld. The bridleway continues through the gorge and follows the river to a bridge on the road at Ivelet. Tan Hill Inn can be reached by taking the road from Muker via Stonesdale; this in turn gives access to 7 miles of good off road riding over moorland and through spectacular river scenery.

Route Description

Leave Muker on the B6270 and follow it W then N for 4m through Thwaite, Angram and Keld to pickup the Tan Hill road at Park Bridge just down stream from Wainwath Force. Turn R and cross Park Bridge; follow the road N for 4m as it climbs up Stonesdale to Tan Hill and the Tan Hill Inn.

Opposite the Tan Hill Inn a track heads S across the moors. Follow it as it makes a short climb to a junction. Take the R fork and continue S along the deteriorating track. The track is well used and easy to follow (part of the Pennine Way) but is very boggy. From the high point just past the junction the track starts to descend, continue along it as it swings round to the SW over Stonesdale Moor. After 1m the track spilts again; the R fork drops down to the road; take the L fork which climbs slightly. Continue S for 2¼m to East Stonesdale Farm passing through a rough section of walled lane near Frith Lodge then finishing with a steep descent.

Pass straight through East Stonesdale Farm and make a short steep descent down the track to a junction. Take the L fork and follow the track over East Gill and up the hill on the other side. Just round the corner is Kisdon Force an impressive waterfall that is easily reached by a short walk. From Kisdon Force follow the track SW then S through the huge gorge formed by the River Swale to Ramps Holme Farm. Along a rocky terrace for the first 1m the track then drops down to the valley floor. From Ramps Holme Farm continue a short distance along the track to a junction. Take the L fork and follow W to join a road which leads in 1½ miles down into Ivelet. From Ivelet backtrack E and cross the River Swale to join the B6270; turn R and follow it for 1½m back to Muker.

Old Gang Smelting Mills

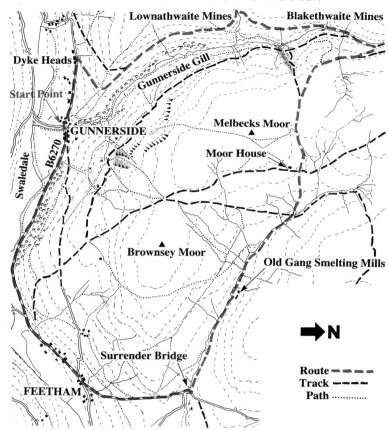

Gunnerside Gill and Old Gang Beck

Grade: Moderate - Time: 3½ Hours - Height Gain: 1150ft
Distance: 11 Miles - 6½ off road, 4½ on road
Terrain: Valleys and high moorland
Surface: Gravelly mining tracks and roads
Start Point Grid Reference: 951982, Gunnerside
Maps: O.S. Yorkshire Dales 1:25 000 Northern Area, Landranger 91 & 98
1:50 000

The wild wind-swept moors north of Gunnerside in Swaledale were once busy with lead mining. Now abandoned these mines have left a legacy of ruined workings, spoil heaps and a network of tracks. Time and the elements have taken their toll mellowing the workings to become an integral part of this fascinating landscape. The numerous access tracks give easy mountain bike riding over well-graded routes. There are two main areas of interest; Gunnerside Gill and Old Gang Beck. The best approach is along Gunnerside Gill from the head of which a bridleway connects with the head of Old Gang Beck. The bridleway which links the two is ill-defined and steep at first forcing a carry; but don't let this put you off, because the carry is short, and the splendid 3 mile run down Old Gang is well worth it!

Route Description

From the centre of Gunnerside take the minor road that climbs to the W and follow it for ½m to a row of cottages at Dyke Heads. Opposite the cottages there is a track which climbs NE up the fellside. Follow the track which is steep at first but which soon eases as it rounds a ridge and enters Gunnerside Gill. The track then swings round to the NW and climbs steadily above Gunnerside Gill (more a valley than a gill). The riding is easy and leads in 1½m to a bridge and junction at Botcher Gill. Take the R fork and continue to contour above Gunnerside Gill. The track becomes narrower and is followed for 1m through old mine workings to another junction below a steep bluff. The situation here is quite impressive - steep sided streams converge at a series of waterfalls amongst abandoned mine bulidings. Take the R fork which follows the course of Gunnerside Gill for ½m. The route now backtracks and traverses the steep hill side to the E. There are numerous routes up the hill side; some of them false and all of them steep which will after 300ft lead to a good access track.

The access track is clear on the ground and heads S then E over Melbecks Moor. Follow it as it climbs through an area of gravel spoil heaps to a high point near a line of shooting butts. From the high point continue E as the track starts to descend for 1m to a bridge - this is Level House Bridge. Cross the bridge and continue along the track down Old Gang Beck. The track follows Old Gang Beck for 2m past old mine buildings to the road at Surrender Bridge giving a fast descent over easy terrain. At the road turn R and follow S up a short climb and then make the descent down into Feetham. From Feetham take B6270 W back to Gunnerside.

Overleaf left: Bridge at North Hush, Gunnerside Gill.

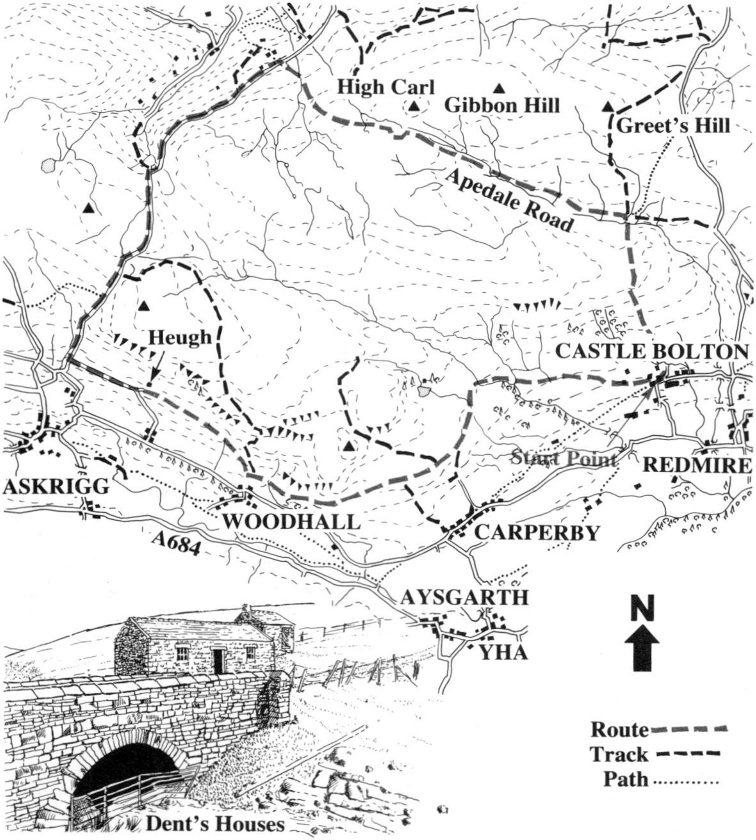

Dent's Houses

Apedale Road

Grade: Moderate - Time: 3½-4 Hours - Height Gain: 1575ft
Distance: 15 Miles - 11½ off road, 3½ on road
Terrain: Moorland and low fells
Surface: Farm tracks, steep roads and stony access tracks
Start Point Grid Reference: 033911, Castle Bolton
Maps: O.S. Yorkshire Dales 1:25 000 Central and Northern Area, Landranger 98 1:50 000

Overleaf right: Looking toward High Carl from Fleak Moss.

The Apedale Road is one of those wonderful rare routes over high terrain that can be ridden along the whole of its course. It is more usual with routes of this type amongst hilly or mountainous terrain, that a large proportion of the time is spent pushing or carrying your bike no matter how skilled a rider you are.

Apedale is a high valley on the moors between Swaledale and Wensleydale. The Apedale road climbs from Swaledale up Whitaside Moor to Apedale Head, it then drops into Apedale and down to Dent's Houses. Throughout its length the road is well used and easy to follow and provides a particularly fast run on the first part of the descent into Apedale. A good place to start this route is at Castle Bolton; this being the medieval castle ruin in Wensleydale. A bridleway starts just behind the castle and heads west along the side of Wensleydale through grassy pasture for 6 miles. It then joins the Swaledale road which leads after some steep climbing to the start of the Apedale Road.

Route Description

Take the track that starts on the N side of Castle Bolton and follow it W for 4m to a ford. The track crosses pasture land and is both easy to ride and easy to follow as it maintains a consistent height and is clear on the ground. After 1½m it swings round to the S but soon returns to its W course as it rounds the flank of a hill. Once the ford is crossed enter a walled lane and follow it to a junction. Turn L, then make an immediate R turn to join another track. Follow the track W as it climbs then levels to join a lane after 1½m. Continue W along the lane to join a road which goes over to Swaledale. Turn R and follow the road for 4m to the start of a bridleway. The road climbs steeply for 1½m to the top of a pass which gives superb views over Swaledale; the descent on the other side is fast and has a couple of sharp bends!

The bridleway starts on the R of the road high above a group of farm houses. Follow it SE as it climbs Whitaside Moor towards High Carl. The bridleway is steep but ridable for 1½m through some old mine workings to a fence and gate near a big hole. This is the high point and the start of the Apedale road. Follow the road SE down Apedale for 2¼m to a junction near Dent's Houses (shooting lodge). At the junction turn R and follow the good track as it climbs S to cross a low ridge line, with a gate on the crest. Pass through the gate and descend the deteriorating track down over pasture land then along a lane to Castle Bolton.

Castle Bolton

The Cam High Road near Wether Fell

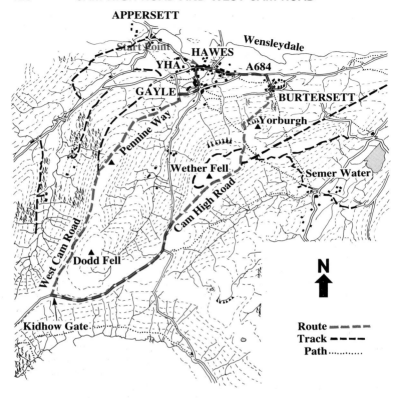

Cam High Road and West Cam Road

Grade: Moderate - Time: 3 ½ Hours - Height Gain: 1325ft
Distance: 11 Miles - 7 ½ off road, 3 ½ on road
Terrain: Open moorland and low fells
Surface: Roads, steep rutted bridleway and stony drove roads
Start Point Grid Reference: 872898, Hawes
Maps: O.S. Yorkshire Dales 1:25 000 Western and Central Areas, Landranger 98 1:50 000

The Roman Roads that cross the Yorkshire Dales in unrelenting straight lines have fortunately not all been adopted as roads. Many, particularly those over higher ground have been left alone, and are now very popular with walkers and riders. One example of this that is particularly good for mountain biking, is the Cam High Road which starts at Bainbridge in Wensleydale, and heads south west towards Cam Fell. An excellent tour can be had by taking the steep bridleway from Burtersett and joining Cam High Road at Wether Hill and then following it across the moors to Kidhow Gate. This then gives access to a lofty section of track known as the West Cam Road. Part of the Pennine Way, the West Cam Road is level until it reaches Ten End; after which it makes a steep and bumpy descent back to Wensleydale.

Route Description

From Hawes take the A684, E for 1m to the Burtersett turning. Turn R and cycle through to a junction at the top of the village. Turn L and follow the road a short distance to the side of some farm buildings and the start of a bridleway. The bridleway climbs steeply S, then zig-zags SW up the hill side. Continue up it as it swings S around the base of Yorburgh until the gradient eases on the E flank of Wether Hill. Make another steep climb and then cross a peaty plateau until after a total 1¾m, Cam High Road is reached. The route up and across the flank of Wether Hill is not clear on the ground - maintain a generally S course and avoid the difficult terrain near the summit.

Cam High Road is a walled lane which is easy to ride along and affords excellent views of the surrounding valleys. Follow it SW with a fast stony descent down to the road. Join the road (actually the continuation of Cam High Road) and follow it SW to a junction. Continue straight (SW) across the junction; and following the road easily for 2½m to Kidhow Gate.

Kidhow Gate marks the junction with West Cam Road which is followed NE back towards Hawes. This section of the West Cam Road is part of the Pennine Way and provides a lovely route which is absolutely ideal for mountain bikes high above the valley of Snaizeholme. The first 2½m follow a well graded and walled terrace across the steep NW side of Dodd Fell to a junction at Ten End. At the junction take the R fork and continue along the Pennine Way; the original route of the West Cam Road goes L. After the junction the track climbs slightly before dropping straight down the hillside giving some steep, testing riding for 2m with plenty of rocks and holes to catch out the unwary. Join the road and follow it first L then R through junctions and down into Gayle. Continue through Gayle and then head back to Hawes.

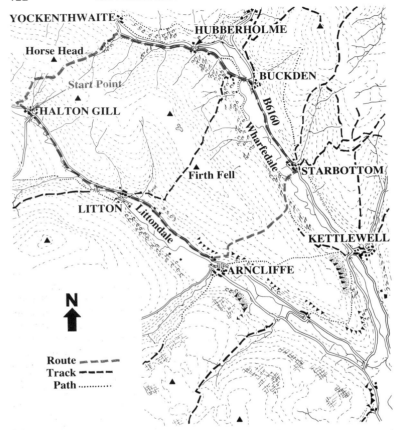

Littondale and Wharfedale

Grade: Difficult - Time: 3½ Hours - Height Gain: 2175ft
Distance: 13½ Miles - 5 off road, 8½ on road
Terrain: Valleys and high fells
Surface: Steep fell tracks, boggy bridleway, road and terraced bridleway
Start Point Grid Reference: 879767, Halton Gill
Maps: O.S. Yorkshire Dales 1:25 000 Central Area, Landranger 98 1:50 000

Throughout the Yorkshire Dales, the number of rights of way that go to, or near to, the summits are few and far between. One such exception is the system of bridleways that crosses the long ridge formed by Horse Head and Firth Fell. The ridge divides Littondale from Wharefdale maintaining a constant height of around 2000ft for 3 miles, and is crossed by bridleways at three points. The two most favourable bridleways cross the ridge at Horse Head and Old Cote Moor. If you start at Halton Gill and follow the route in a clock-wise direction both bridleways give a well graded ascent and an exciting descent. Generally the going is good, over firm rocky tracks and grass; but the start of the descent from Horse Head is very boggy requiring care to avoid erosion.

Route Description

From the W side of Halton Gill take the good track that climbs the fell side to the N. The track gains hight through a series of zig-zags and after 1m crosses a ford. After the ford the gradient relents making the riding/push-ing easier. Continue E along the track for ½m to a gate on the crest of the ridge. This is Horse Head Gate - the summit of Horse Head is ¼m to the NW along the ridge. The descent from Horse Head Gate is to the NE and is clear on the ground. The first section is very boggy and in many places resmbles a stream more than a path; so take care not to make matters worse. Things get better after the ford at Hagg Beck; the ground steepens and becomes much firmer giving an exciting run down through a series of bends until the road is reached near Yockenthwaite. At the road, turn R and follow it down the valley and past Hubberhlome to join the B6160 at Buckden, in Wharfed-ale. Turn R and follow the B6160 S along Wharfedale for 2m to Starbotton.

   Continue through Starbotton and take the bridleway on the R as soon as you leave the village. Follow the bridleway for a short distance to a ford (foot bridge). Cross the river, and continue along the lane which is quite rough but soon leads to a terraced track which climbs S up the valley side. Follow the terrace for ½m first through the trees then over open fell until it swings round to the SW and climbs directly up the hill side (don't continue along the path). The track climbs steeply for ½m until it reaches the crest of the ridge running down from Firth Fell. From the ridge the track descends gently at first towards the W but soon steepens giving an excellent down hill run. Follow it over firm grass; then along a rocky access track for 1½m down into Littondale. Turn R onto the valley road and follow it NW for 4½m through Litton to return to Halton Gill.

The climb out of Wharfedale

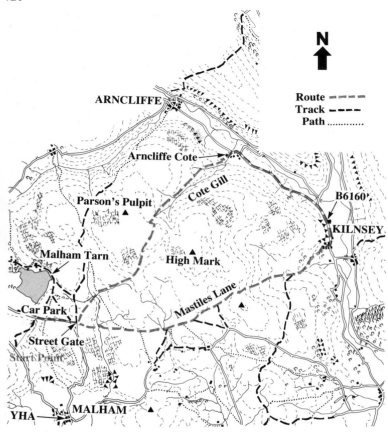

Mastiles Lane

Grade: Moderate - Time: 3 Hours - Height Gain: 1200ft
Distance: 13 Miles - 9 off road, 4 on road
Terrain: Limestone moorland
Surface: Road, grassy track and rutted drove road
Start Point Grid Reference: 895658, car park S of Malham Tarn
Maps: O.S. Yorkshire Dales 1:25 000 Southern Area, Landranger 98 1:50 000

Mastiles Lane was originally a monastic track which linked the Malham estates of Fountains Abbey with a 'Grange' (monastic farm) at Kilnsey. Still in regular use as a green road it provides a scenic and direct route between Kilnsey and Street Gate on the Malham road. Also joining the Malham road at Street Gate is another track which follows a more northerly but parallel course to Mastiles Lane. The track climbs to Lee Gate High Mark and then descends alongside the impressive valley formed by Cote Gill to Arncliffe Cote in Littondale. Both routes provide excellent mountain biking terrain which is nowhere particularly difficult but always interesting. The two routes can be linked by taking the road along Littondale under the huge overhang of Kilnsey Crag back to Kilnsey to complete an enjoyable round-tour.

Route Description

From the car park near Malham Tarn outlet turn L onto the road and follow it E for ½m to Street Gate. On the other side of the gate there are two tracks; the one going E is Mastiles Lane (return route), the other heads NE. Take the NE track and follow it as it descends to a ford. Cross the ford and continue along the track first N then NE as it begins to climb. After ½m it steepens and swings round to the N again at a ridge line below some crags. Traverse N below the crags until the gradient levels and the track splits. Take the R fork, and head NE passing through a series of walls. Continue along the track as it begins to descend into the head of Cote Gill. The track follows a course high along the NW side of Cote Gill and gives a fast run down over firm grass. After 1½m the track enters a rocky lane which leads in a short distance to the road at Arncliffe Cote in Littondale.

From Arncliffe Cote turn R and follow the road SE to join B6160. Turn R onto the B6160 S for 1m to Kilnsey, passing under the huge overhang of Kilnsey Crag. Mastiles Lane starts in Kilnsey and can be found just behind the hotel.

Turn R off the B6160 between the hotel and houses. The first section of Mastiles Lane is metalled and climbs steeply round a bend past a quarry. Continue straight past the quarry entrance to a junction; take the R fork and continue W along the walled part of the lane. The next section climbs steadily to the highest part of Mastiles Lane at Holgates Kilnsey Moor a gain of 500ft in 1m - the surface is good so it can be ridden all the way. From Holgates Kilnsey Moor descend SW along the lane to Mastiles Gate. Past Mastiles Gate the surface deteriorates into a sticky morass caused by vehicle tracks - route finding is not a problem, just follow the ruts. Continue

W along the lane for 2½m as it slowly descends to a ford. There is a steep hill down to the ford which gives just about the right momentum to cross it; so long as you are fast enough! Street Gate is up the hill on the other side and ½m W along the track.

Kilnsey Old Hall

The ford on Mastiles Lane

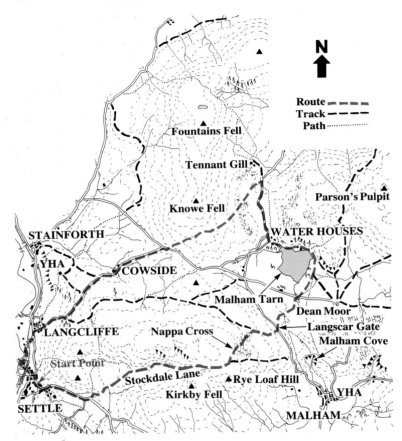

Malham Tarn from Settle

Grade: Moderate - **Time:** 4 Hours - **Height Gain:** 1700ft
Distance: 14 Miles - 8 off road, 6 on road
Terrain: Limestone Moorland
Surface: Road, indistinct bridleway over grassy moorland, access road and stony drove road
Start Point Grid Reference: 819638, Settle
Maps: O.S. Yorkshire Dales 1:25 000 Southern Area, Landranger 98 1:50 000

Any guide book to the Yorkshire Dales would be incomplete without a route that included the outstanding limestone scenery around Malham. There are caves, dry valleys, gorges and pavements; but the jewel in the crown has to be Malham Cove. This mighty natural amphitheatre was formed by the erosive action of glacial outwash which, after receding, left a crag of nearly 300ft in height - now a popular venue for rock gymnasts. As with the rest of the Dales the area is well endowed with bridleways and drove roads. Malham Tarn can be reached from Settle by taking the road through Langcliffe and then up to Henside, from where a little-used bridleway leads over Malham Moor. From the tarn another bridleway heads south and connects with Stockdale Lane, an excellent drove road, which leads back towards Settle. Malham Cove and Watlowes (dry valley) lie due south of the first part of the return leg, but they can only be visited on foot - so make sure you take a good bike lock with you.

Route Description

From the centre of Settle take the A65 W; then pick up the B6479 at a junction near the bridge over the River Ribble. Follow the B6479 for ¾m to a junction at Langcliffe. Turn R onto the Malham road and follow it for 3m as it climbs steeply through a series of bends, then more steadily past a farm at Cowside and on to a T junction at Henside. Directly opposite the junction, a bridleway starts, and heads NE across Malham Moor (stile opposite junction; gate L, further down the road). The bridleway is difficult to follow being indistinct on the ground; its course is straight and climbs steadily for 1m on a bearing of 67° (grid) to a low col amongst a patch of exposed limestone pavement - gates through walls and fences are not in line on this section of the bridleway. From the col the bridleway descends NE and becomes more obvious, giving a good 1½m descent over pleasant pasture down to the road. Turn R, and follow it S for 1m, until it is possible to turn L and pick up a track at Water Houses that leads to Malham Tarn House. This beautiful country house overlooking Malham Tarn is now a field study centre and makes a great lunch stop.

From Malham Tarn House follow the track S as it skirts around the tarn, and pick up the bridleway which heads SW across pleasant grassland (not the Pennine Way) to a road which crosses the outlet stream from Malham Tarn. Take the road across the stream; then make an immediate L off it to join another bridleway. The bridleway crosses Dean Moor; follow it SW for ¾m to Langscar Gate and the Malham Cove road. At this point you can make a slight detour; either ride down the road to Malham Cove, or leave your bike and walk down Watlowes dry valley to the top of Malham Cove - which should be approached with caution; or you may end up making 'one giant step for mountain bikers'!

On the opposite side of the road at Langscar Gate, is a track; follow it by a wall and then through an old sheep pen as it climbs W, then SW for 1m to Nappa Cross (the position of which is marked by a stone column in a wall). From Nappa Cross a short ride S along the wall leads to Stockdale Lane and a cairn at its highest point - also the highest point on this route. Follow Stockdale Lane as it heads W giving a 2½m down hill run, with lots of rock steps and bumps, to a road junction. Turn R and follow the road back to Settle with a fine steep hill straight down into the town.

Fasten all gates

Fountains Fell and Malham from Kirkby Fell

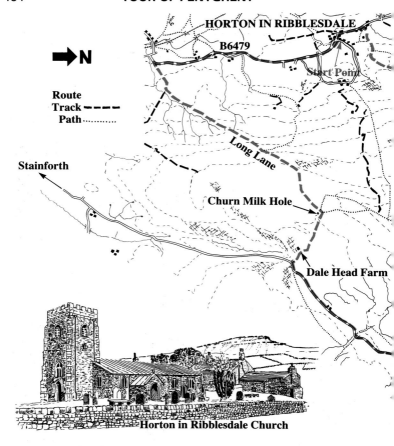

➡N

Route
Track — — —
Path ....

HORTON IN RIBBLESDALE

B6479

Start Point

Long Lane

Stainforth

Churn Milk Hole

Dale Head Farm

Horton in Ribblesdale Church

Tour of Penyghent

Grade: Difficult - Time: 3½-4 hours - Height Gain: 1225ft
Distance: 14 Miles - 9 off road, 5 on road
Terrain: High moorland
Surface: Steep rough lanes, boggy moorland, high pasture and roads
Start Point Grid Reference: 807726, Horton in Ribblesdale
Maps: O.S. Yorkshire Dales 1:25 000 Western Area, Landrange 98 1:50 000

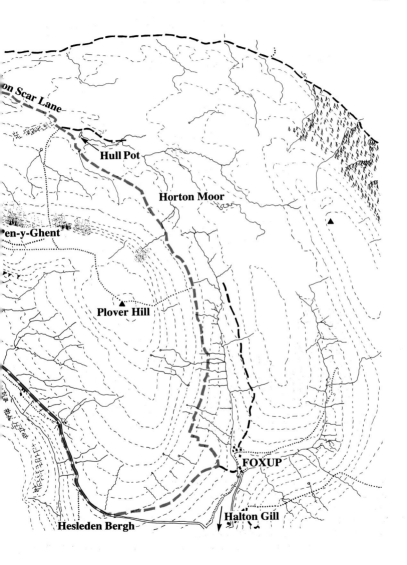

on Scar Lane

Hull Pot

Horton Moor

en-y-Ghent

Plover Hill

FOXUP

Halton Gill

Hesleden Bergh

Penyghent, one of the 'Three Peaks' and the first real mountain encountered on the Pennine Way; is unfortunately out of bounds to mountain bikers. The nearest you can get to Penyghent's summit on a bicycle is by taking Horton Scar Lane to Horton Moor. Although only second best to attaining the summit, it is well worth making a tour around Penyghent. All its aspects can be viewed by continuing from Horton Moor along a bridleway to Hesleden Bergh and then along the road to Dale Head Farm and on down to Horton-in-Ribblesdale via Long Lane. The off road riding is excellent the only exception being an area of boggy ground on Horton Moor. Do not let wet weather put you off this tour; if you are lucky and enough rain has fallen Hull Pot will be in a spectacular state.

Route Description

Leave Horton in Ribblesdale along Horton Scar Lane which starts slightly S of and opposite the Penyghent Cafe on the B6479 (Pennine Way sign). Follow Horton Scar Lane 1½m as it climbs a well graded course first E then NE to Horton Moor. The lane is a popular approach route to Penyghent and although steep and loose in parts it can be ridden along its entirety. As the gradient eases the lane reaches a gate and junction. Three tracks leave the gate; to the R is the 'highway' up Penyghent (recently resurfaced), to the L is an access track; take the middle course which heads NE past Hull Pot. Care should be taken when approaching Hull Pot particularly in poor visibility as the track passes very close to it. Skirt round Hull Pot and continue NE along the track which steadily climbs alongside a wall. Easy but boggy riding leads in 1½m to Swarth Gill Gate.

Go through the gate and follow the track as it begins to descend across the NW flank of Plover Hill; the going becomes less boggy as a series of walls is passed. After 2m the track turns down hill (N) and starts to zig-zag down towards Foxup. Just before Foxup is reached backtrack and follow the vague track S as it climbs across the fellside to the road at Hesleden Bergh. This track does climb slightly, but it is better than the long climb you would have to make along the road from Foxup.

From Hesleden Bergh follow the road SW for 3m to Dale Head where the Pennine Way crosses it. Turn R off the road and follow the course of the Pennine Way NW along the track to a junction at Churn Milk Hole. Turn L and leave the Pennine Way and follow the track which climbs slightly then descends to the SW. This is Long Lane which gives an excellent 2¼m run down to the main Ribblesdale road. Join the B6479 and follow it back to Horton in Ribblesdale.

Hull Pot on the Tour of Penyghent

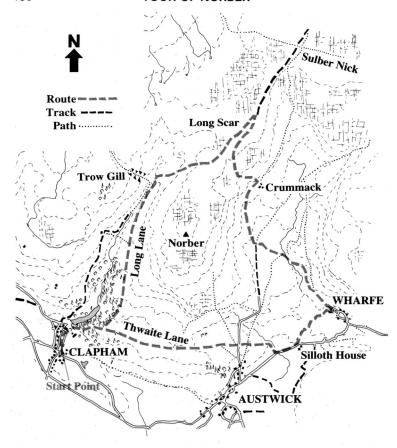

Tour of Norber

Grade: Easy - Time: 1½ - Height Gain: 740ft
Distance: 7½ Miles - 6½ off road, 1 on road
Terrain: Limestone moorland
Surface: Rough lanes, quiet road and grassy moorland
Start Point Grid Reference: 746694, Clapham
Maps: O.S. Yorkshire Dales 1:25 000 Western Area, Landranger 98 1:50 000

Finding a mountain bike route that is both interesting and easy, particularly for beginners is no easy task. The structure of hilly or mountainous areas tends to dictate long valleys and ridges that are not easily crossed, easy terrain tends to be limited to the valley bottoms. One such area of high ground that does contain easy riding terrain and much interest is the limestone upland of Norber, Sulber and Crummack Dale above Clapham. A short tour of the area can be made by taking Thwaite Lane out of Clapham and returning along Long Lane from Sulber. Both lanes are walled tracks and provide excellent going - Long lane is particularly good in descent.

Route Description

The start of this route is quite unusual, being subterranean in nature. On the E side of the church in Clapham is the entrance to a tunnel formed by two long spans which carry private roads. Follow the track (Thwaite Lane) through the tunnel as it climbs away from the village. After ¼m another track, Long Lane, joins it on the L - this is the return route. Pass the junction and continue along Thwaite Lane. Pleasant, easy riding, leads in 1½m to a junction with a road. Turn L and follow the road E for ¼m to the start of a bridleway that leaves the road on the L, at Silloth House. Follow the bridleway as it climbs NE into Wharfe. Take the lane that leaves Wharfe on the N side and follow it as it climbs steadily to the NW. After ¾m it reaches a ford; cross the ford and follow the lane on the other side to a junction. Turn R and follow the lane N to the farm at Crummack. Just the other side of the farm a bridleway climbs the hill side to the W. The bridleway is not too clear on the ground but it follows a course roughly parallel to the wall gradually bending round to the N until after ¾m it breaks out on to a level area amongst limestone pavements. This is the high point of the route and is midway along a low ridge between Norber and Sulber.

Back tracking on the other side of the ridge another bridleway gradually descends SW (cairns) towards the head of Clapdale. Follow it over easy grass and outcrops for 1m through a gate to another gate and sheep pen at the head of a lane. This is the top of Long Lane which gives an exhilarating descent particularly amongst the loose rocks at the start. After 1½m and a short climb to finish, Long Lane connects with Thwaite Lane. Turn L and follow it back through the tunnel to Clapham - remember to take your sunglasses off before you enter the tunnel! On the other side of Clapdale from Long Lane is Ingelborough Cave and Trow Gill which are well worth a visit. A bridleway runs up from Clapham; Trow Gill is a short walk further on.

Good equipment and clothing are essential

Clapdale and Norber from Thwaite Lane

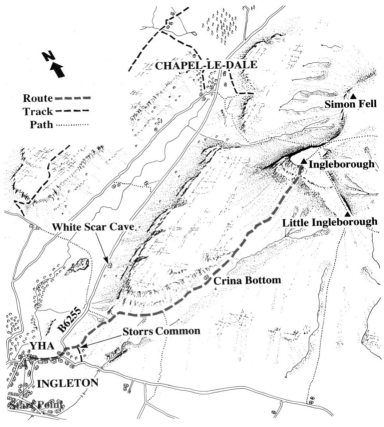

N

Route ▬ ▬ ▬
Track ▬ ▬ ▬
Path ∙∙∙∙∙∙∙∙∙∙

CHAPEL-LE-DALE

Simon Fell ▲

▲ Ingleborough

White Scar Cave

▲ Little Ingleborough

Crina Bottom

B6255

Storrs Common

YHA

INGLETON

Sart Point

Ingleborough

Grade: Very Difficult - Time: 2-2½ Hours - Height Gain: 1950ft
Distance: 6½ Miles - 5½ off road, 1 on road
Terrain: Limestone moorland and high fell
Surface: Muddy rutted lane, peaty moorland and steep crags below the summit
Sart Point Grid Reference: 696732, Ingleton.
Maps: O.S. Yorkshire Dales 1:25 000 Western Area, Landranger 98 1:50 000

Ingleborough is one of those hills that is popular because of its distinctive shape. Isolated and in a dominant position, its flat summit and stepped crags are easily identified from all directions and over a considerable distance. Its summit has been home to a native settlement and a Hill Fort, the remains of which can still be seen. Access for mountain bikers is limited to a bridleway that climbs directly to the summit from Ingleton. The bridleway was probably the historic route up Ingleborough, and follows the easiest approach possible, the only difficulties occur at the stepped crags just below the summit. In descent, once the stepped crags have been passed, the route is excellent - a combination of fast grassy sections and rutted rocky areas.

Route Description

Take the B6255 as it climbs, E out of Ingelton for ½m passing the Clapham turning to Storrs Common. At Storrs Common turn R off the B6255 and join Fell Lane. At the top of the common the Fell Lane becomes walled and is followed for 1½m as it climbs to Crina Bottom. The lane is very rough but is ridable. Continue NW past the cottage at Crina Bottom and follow the eroded path over a series of rock steps to a level area near area of shake holes (Quaking Pot). This marks the start of the final and steepest part of the ascent, which climbs straight up the SW slope of Ingleborough. As the summit is neared the track climbs through two outcrops of rock which can be awkward especialy in a strong wind. The summit shelter, trig point and cairn are just over the top of the second outcrop.

The huge flat summit of Ingleborough is worth exploring as there are still the remains of a hill fort and settlement scattered about (this hill fort is a scheduled Ancient Monument, and it is illegal to cycle anywhere on the summit plateau other than on the public bridleway). The return leg follows the ascent route so requires no description other than don't attempt to ride down the summit crags - quite a few 'Three Peaks' competitors have tried it and soon come unstuck!

Overleaf left: Descending Ingleborough's summit crags.

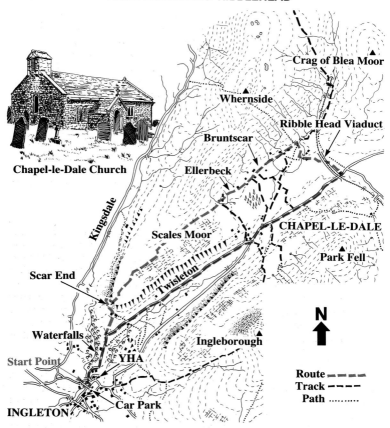

Crag of Blea Moor ▲

▲ **Whernside**

Ribble Head Viaduct

Bruntscar

Ellerbeck

Chapel-le-Dale Church

Scales Moor

CHAPEL-LE-DALE

Park Fell ▲

Kingsdale

Scar End

Twisleton

▲ **Ingleborough**

Waterfalls

Start Point

YHA

Car Park

INGLETON

N

Route — — —
Track - - - -
Path ....

Twisleton and Ribblehead

Grade: Moderate - Time: 2-2 ½ Hours - Height Gain: 900ft
Distance: 13 Miles - 6 off road, 7 on road
Terrain: Limestone moorland and high pasture
Surface: Steep loose ascent, limestone pavement, farm tracks and quiet single track roads
Start Point Grid Reference: 696732, Ingleton
Maps: O.S. Yorkshire Dales 1:25 000 Western Area, Landranger 98 1:50 000

Overleaf left: Ford at Ellerbeck; Ingleborough beyond.

Whernside's south west ridge extends for over 5 miles to terminate at Scar End a craggy bluff between the River Doe and the River Greta just above Ingleton. The two sides of the ridge differ - to the north west steep uniform slopes descend into Kingsdale; whilst to the south east, the slopes are punctuated by a ½ mile wide limestone plateau edged by the crags of Twisleton Scars. Traversing the plateau is a bridleway which starts at Scar End, crosses the limestone pavement of Scales Moor and then passes through the farms at Ellerbeck, Bruntscar and Ivescar to come out at the Ribblehead Viaduct. As a mountain bike ride the plateau is not particularly difficult, being easily accessible and relatively level: its attraction lies in the ever changing scenery and numerous obstacles to be overcome; of which the hardest is a short steep scramble up Scar End - the only unridable section! This route is best attempted in clear weather as the views of Ingleborough are quite spectacular and the navigation on Scales Moor can be quite frustrating in poor visibility.

Route Description

From the centre of Ingleton, cross the bridge over the River Doe then turn immediate R and follow the road past the gas holder. This is Oddies Lane, steep at first; follow it for 1m until it is possible to take a farm track on the L (at a bend). Follow the track through the farm at Twisleton Hall until, after 300yds past the farm, a bridleway zig-zags up the steep hillside on the R. The bridleway climbs over a scree fan to the base of a short crag. The crag can be overcome by following the wall or by scrambling through a narrow gully in front of the crag (both routes are well trodden). From the top of the crag head NE for ½m, roughly parallel with the wall to a cairn and shelter - the highest point on the route.

From the shelter the bridleway continues NE for 2½m across Scales Moor to a ford at Ellerbeck Gill, gradually losing height all the time. The riding is easy, but not without entertainment, as you will need to carefully pick your way through the limestone pavement; the best routes are not always the most obvious. Cross the ford and continue NE along a short lane to the farm at Ellerbeck - after Ellerbeck the route crosses enclosed farmland so be careful to stay on the right of way. Pass straight through the farm and pick up a track which crosses another ford and leads after ½m to a lane and farms at Bruntscar. From Bruntscar the bridleway still heads NE but is more clear on the ground. Follow it for 1½m over more pasture land to pick up a lane past houses and farms; then make a R turn on to the tarmac road SE towards the Ribblehead Viaduct. After ¼m turn L and cross the bridge over Winterscales Beck. Take the track under the viaduct and follow it to the main road. Turn R and follow the main road for 2m S to Chapel-le-Dale. Turn R and take Oddies Lane for 4m back to Ingleton.

Typical limestone pavement

The Ribble Head Viaduct at the start of Craven Old Way

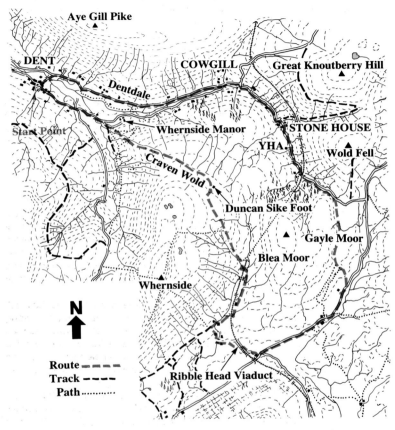

Craven Old Way

Grade: Difficult - Time: 4 hours - Height Gain: 1730ft
Distance: 17½ Miles - 7½ off road, 10 on road
Terrain: Valley and exposed moorland
Surface: Steep and narrow roads, farm tracks and boggy moorland
Start Point Grid Reference: 705870, Dent
Maps: O.S. Yorkshire Dales 1:25 000 Western Area, Landranges 98 1:50 000

The Craven Old Way is a Drove Road between Dent and Ingleton that crosses the northern flank of Whernside. It starts at Ribble Head Viaduct, and winds its way up past the fantastically engineered entrance to Bleamoor Railway Tunnel: to a height of 1750ft at Duncan Sike Foot. It then descends to Dentdale, giving an exciting but damp 2½m down hill run. To start the route, pleasantly quiet roads through Dent, and Dentdale can be followed towards Ribblehead. Before the main Ribble Head road is reached it is possible to join a section of the Dales Way. At first the track seems harmless enough but it soon deteriorates into a boggy morass in which you can guarantee to get soaked. The worst sections have duck boards which can provide much entertainment - especially if you slip off into the awaiting gunge! The road is then joined to Ribbleshead which gives access to the Craven Old Way.

Route Description

Two roads run along Dentdale one S of the River Dee and one N. Take the N road out of Dent which crosses the river and follow it E for 6½m. The last 1¼m of the road past Stone House climbs steeply up out of Dentdale. As the road levels a bridleway leaves it on the R (Dales Way sign); turn R onto it and follow it S across moorland. There is some height gain but the biggest problem is staying dry. After 1m the track splits; take the L fork and follow it down to the Ribble Head road. Turn R and follow the road SW to Ribblehead.

From the road, on the NE side of the railway line, a track leaves the road. Turn R, off the road and follow the track under the viaduct. Continue along the track to a T junction over a bridge, by a farm. Turn R and follow a section of metalled road to another T junction. Turn R and follow the track NE towards the railway line and through a farm. Continue along the track and go through the tunnel. On the other side of the railway line follow it for 1m to a bridge that carries a stream; cross over the bridge.

The Craven Old Way climbs straight up the hill side to the NW for 1½m to Craven Wold - it is consistently steep and very boggy and can be monotonous in mist. Just over the crest of the ridge, formed by Craven Wold, is Duncan Sike Foot, a ruined shooting lodge where the track splits. Take the track on the L side of the building and follow it N then NW to join a walled lane, descend along it then follow the track down ridge and stream to Dentdale. Turn L along the Whernside Manor lane and join the road. Turn R onto the road and follow it a short distance to the main road; which is followed W back to Dent

The track toward High Pike - the Howgills in the far distance

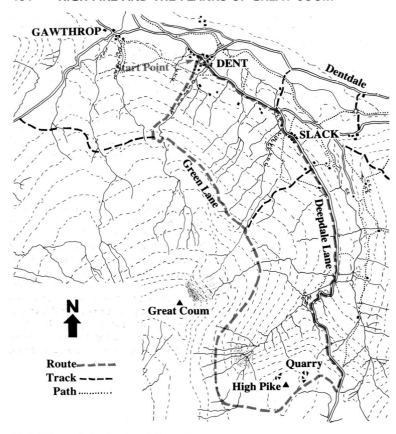

High Pike and the flanks of Great Coum

Grade: Moderate - Time: 2½ Hours - Height Gain: 1060ft
Distance: 8½ Miles - 5 off road, 3½ on road
Terrain: Valley and high moorland
Surface: Steep narrow roads, rutted boggy track, stony track and a loose descent
Start Point Grid Reference: 705870, Dent
Maps: O.S. Yorkshire Dales 1:25 000 Western Area, Landranger 98 1:50 000

The Drove Roads and Green Roads of the Yorkshire Dales are generally in good order, presenting no real technical problems for a mountain biker. There are of course always exceptions; of which one is Green Lane, a track which contours around the north eastern side of Great Coum above Dent. Easy access to Green Lane can be had from the road at the head of Kingsdale; which has encouraged use by the four wheel drive fraternity. The first section past the old quarry at High Pike has escaped undamaged, but after this the track is deeply rutted and corrugated providing very testing mountain bike riding for 3 miles. A short easy section follows this with great views over Dentdale, before the fast rocky descent into Dent, which is down a steep walled track amongst overhanging trees. For those who enjoy a technical challenge without too much work this route is a must.

Route Description

From Dent there are two roads up Dentdale one N of the River Dee and one S. Take the S road and follow it for 1m to a junction. Turn R at the junction and follow it for 3m to the top of the pass over into Kingsdale.

The start of Green Lane is actually just below the top of the pass on the Dentdale side. Turn R onto it and follow it as it climbs NW then SW just below the old quarry on High Pike. Continue along the track as it contours around High Pike and heads W across moorland and becomes boggy. After a ford the track swings round to the N and descends slowly across the exposed flanks of Great Coum providing testing riding among the rocks, ruts and mud. 2m from the ford the track splits at a junction; take the L fork and follow the track more easily as it descends SW for 1½m to another junction. This time turn R and follow the fast stony track straight down along side a stream to Dent.

Useful Addresses

British Mountaineering Council
Crawford House
Precinct Centre
Booth Street East
Manchester
M13 9RZ
Telephone: 061-273 5835

Cross-Country Cycling Club
5 Station Road
Ford
West Sussex

Cyclist's Touring Club
69 Meadrow
Godalming
Surrey
GU7 3HS
Telephone: 04868 7217

Mountain Bike Club
Santon House
Santon Downham
Suffolk
IP27 0TT

Rough-Stuff Fellowship
9 Liverpool Avenue
Southport
Merseyside
PR8 3NE

Descending toward Settle along Stockdale Lane

MOUNTAIN BIKER

MOUNTAIN
BIKER

*THE MAGAZINE WITH ITS
FINGER ON THE PULSE AND
ITS FEET ON THE PEDALS*

*READ IT EVERY MONTH FOR THE BES
TOURS, TRAINING, RACES REPORTS
AND TECHNICAL FEATURES*

100 PAGES FOR ONLY £1.9

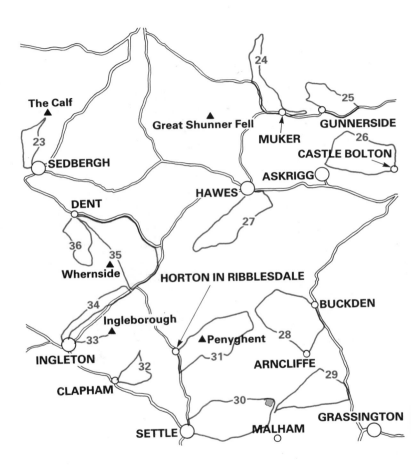

The Calf

Great Shunner Fell

24

25

GUNNERSIDE

23

MUKER

26

SEDBERGH

CASTLE BOLTON

ASKRIGG

HAWES

DENT

27

36

35

Whernside

HORTON IN RIBBLESDALE

BUCKDEN

34

Ingleborough

28

33

Penyghent

31

INGLETON

32

ARNCLIFFE

29

CLAPHAM

30

GRASSINGTON

SETTLE

MALHAM